"Mark's music has mear   of Christ. His life, his faith,   as real as they come. Mark rea   ly ever after—but it's what h   .…at makes his book worth reading. In a style as thoughtful as it is entertaining, he offers great insights on how to stop chasing the 'what's next' and 'what-ifs' in order to experience God right now, even in the midst of a difficult situation."

Candace Cameron Bure, actress and author

"I have spent time with Mark Lee and his family, and he is truly the real deal. The story of his journey in *Hurt Road* will definitely inspire you to take your faith to the next level."

Mark Richt, head coach of the Miami Hurricanes football team

"If you've been blessed and inspired by Third Day's music, as I have for so many years, *Hurt Road* will take you along on Mark Lee's personal journey. Mark shares honestly and openly his heart and how his personal faith has enabled him to overcome some of life's toughest hurdles. We are all different and yet, in many ways, we are the same. There are lessons we can learn from Mark's experiences that can be applied in our lives and our walk with the Lord Jesus. The bottom line is this: if we are truly his children he will never leave us nor forsake us. We can always count on Roman 8:28: "And we know that God causes everything to work together for the good for those who love God and are called according to his purpose.'"

Steve Bartkowski, two-time Pro Bowl quarterback for the Atlanta Falcons

"Each of us has a story to tell, and Mark is kind enough to capture his for us to read. I've known Mark for well over two decades. Each time I am with him, I walk away encouraged and inspired. I'm confident that reading this book will do the same for you."

Max Lucado

"I have shared the stage with Mark Lee many times and have been inspired by his love for God and his genuine love for people. *Hurt Road* is a great read and gave me insights into Mark's life that were fascinating and inspiring. It is a gentle call to a moment-by-moment faith that will continue to resonate with you long after you read the book."

Michael W. Smith

"*Hurt Road* is a fascinating and moving story from my friend Mark Lee. It's one worth picking up, reading for yourself, and then sharing with someone you know would love it too. When people dig into their own story on behalf of the book, it always changes the reader. This book did that for me, and I'm thankful for the hard work Mark did."

Annie F. Downs, bestselling author of *Looking for Lovely* and *Let's All Be Brave*

"Over the past few years, as I've been privileged to get to know Mark Lee, I've been struck by his unassuming, straightforward nature despite significant accomplishment. In *Hurt Road*, as Mark takes us on a journey through his life, we gain insight into how high school friends formed a band that became an industry giant (hint: it's as amazing a story as you'd have imagined). But like the band Third Day, which at its core is a group of men who love Jesus and love to make good music to honor him, Mark's personal story is so much more than the success. Told with characteristic humility seasoned with humor, his recounting of life lessons learned along the way and of a man's maturing faith are challenging and at the same time most encouraging."

George Schroeder, national college football writer, *USA TODAY* Sports Media Group

"Mark takes us all for a walk in *Hurt Road*. I could see the images of people and feel the moments of his story. As I read, I found myself going back to my own story of 'landmarks' that ultimately took me to a place of simple trust and obedience. *Hurt Road* will make you laugh, smile, say 'Oh, I remember that!' and get a bit choked up at times. But most of all, even when your road doesn't always make sense, this book will inspire you to lift your head—and just keep walking."

Pete Hixson, pastor of Polaris Church

"Happily ever after. That's the dream for many from our earliest days, and for most it remains just that—a dream. Mark Lee points toward a different path—more pain, more surprises, more difficulties, more joy, and ultimately more true to life and more fulfilling than even our most perfect dreams. Drawing from his own experiences, Mark serves as an excellent guide for all who find themselves following God down their personal *Hurt Road*."

David Eldridge, pastor of StoneBridge Church, Marietta, Georgia

"I've always been impressed by the talent and creativity of Mark Lee, but to know more of the story of what God has brought him through has left me amazed at both Mark's faith and God's faithfulness."

Laura Story

"I remember being a young, aspiring artist traveling to Atlanta to see a band who was already at the top of the mountain I hoped to soon climb. Third Day was headlining this particular night and I remember being absolutely blown away by the show, the music, and the ministry. Little did I know I would have the honor of calling Mark Lee friend and having the chance to watch and learn from someone who had worked so hard and achieved great success but always stayed humble. This book is going to give you the same window into Mark's world that has blessed me so much. I know these pages and Mark's story will encourage you wherever on this life's road you may find yourself."

Matthew West

"I have been and will be a Third Day fan for life, and getting to know Mark and hearing his story has made me come to love these guys even more. God has brought Mark through much, and his story will remind you of how big our God is!"

Mark Hall, lead singer of Casting Crowns

"For many years I've known Mark Lee as a great guitar player, a great friend, and a truly great man. What I didn't know was what a great storyteller he is! Thank you, Mark, for sharing your story and your journey with us."

Steven Curtis Chapman

"I have known and respected Mark Lee all the way back to the early days of Third Day. He is a monster on guitar with a gentle heart and never lacks passion. It is amazing how God takes us on all kinds of journeys, and Mark's is one that you will want to read about."

TobyMac

HURT ROAD

HURT

ROAD

THE MUSIC, THE MEMORIES, AND THE MILES BETWEEN

Revell

a division of Baker Publishing Group
Grand Rapids, Michigan

© 2017 by Mark Lee

Published by Revell
a division of Baker Publishing Group
P.O. Box 6287, Grand Rapids, MI 49516-6287
www.revellbooks.com

Printed in the United States of America

Library of Congress Cataloging-in-Publication Data
Names: Lee, Mark, 1973– author.
Title: Hurt road : the music, the memories, and the miles between / Mark Lee.
Description: Grand Rapids : Revell, 2017.
Identifiers: LCCN 2017013101 | ISBN 9780800729004 (pbk.)
Subjects: LCSH: Lee, Mark, 1973– | Rock musicians—United States—Biography.
   | Guitarists—United States—Biography. | Christian biography. | Third Day
   (Christian rock group : 1991–) | LCGFT: Autobiographies.
Classification: LCC ML419.L418 A3 2017 | DDC 782.25/164092—dc23
LC record available at https://lccn.loc.gov/2017013101

Unless otherwise indicated, Scripture quotations are from the Holy Bible, New International Version®. NIV®. Copyright © 1973, 1978, 1984, 2011 by Biblica, Inc.™ Used by permission of Zondervan. All rights reserved worldwide. www.zondervan.com

Scripture quotations labeled NKJV are from the New King James Version®. Copyright © 1982 by Thomas Nelson, Inc. Used by permission. All rights reserved.

Scripture quotations labeled GNT are from the Good News Translation—Second Edition. Copyright © 1992 by American Bible Society. Used by permission.

Some names and details have been changed to protect the privacy of the individuals involved.

All photos courtesy of the author.

Published in association with Creative Trust, Inc., 210 Jamestown Park Drive, Suite 200, Brentwood, TN 37027, www.creativetrust .com.

17 18 19 20 21 22 23   8 7 6 5 4 3 2

To Mom: thank you for raising me up in the way I should go. You helped me find the landmarks that would guide me through life: a love for God, a love for books, and a love for music.

To Jimmy: thank you for being the coolest big brother a guy could ever ask for. Without listening to your record collection, riding in your Trans Am, or your general awesomeness, I wouldn't be who I am today.

To Stephanie: it hasn't been happily ever after, but it's been pretty close! Thank you for all the times you believed in me when I didn't believe in myself. Thank you for encouraging me not just to write a book but to write *this* book. You are the best thing that's ever happened to me.

To Abbie: thank you for holding my hand and helping me figure out this daddy thing. You are my joy.

To Kitty: thank you for always reminding me to stop and capture the little moments of life like lightning bugs in a jar. You are my sweet girl.

Finally, I dedicate this book in memory of my dad, James Leonard Lee. Thank you for showing me what brave looks like.

CONTENTS

Foreword by Mac Powell   13

Acknowledgments   17

1. On the Road   21

2. Once Upon a Time   27

3. Questions of Faith   39

4. Landmarks   51

5. When Calling Comes Calling   59

6. Sucker Punch #1   72

7. If I Can Just Get Over This   82

8. Sucker Punch #2   90

9. Crossfade   112

10. High-Wire Act   122

11. Whirlwind   137

Contents

12. Secret Option C   148

13. Fairy Tales Are Just That   159

14. Getting to Where We Need to Be   169

15. Hanging On and Letting Go   179

16. Homesick   192

17. God Bless Me   203

18. It Makes for a Great Story   214

FOREWORD

I met Mark Lee way back in 1989. We were both juniors
at McEachern High School in the little town of Powder
Springs, Georgia, about thirty miles outside of Atlanta. I was
starting my third high school in three years. We had moved
quite a bit with my dad's job, and it wasn't very fun starting over every year of high school—having to say goodbye
to old friends, hopefully meet new friends, and somehow
try to learn to fit in. Mark had come over to my girlfriend's
house to work on a Beta Club project with her and another
one of their friends. I wasn't part of the Beta Club. I wasn't
exactly Beta Club material. But Mark definitely was. It only
takes a few minutes of conversation with Mark for someone
to realize "This guy is pretty smart!"

I remember that he was on crutches. Now, you've got to
realize that this was close to thirty years ago and I've never
claimed to have the best memory, but I don't remember if at
the time I asked him something like "Hey man, what happened to you?" or if I found out later about the circumstances
that you will soon be reading about in his book. But I do

remember thinking *This guy is kind of cool—I wonder if we'll be friends.* Little did I know at the time that God would use this high school kid to change my life and set us both on a course to allow us to not only chase our dreams but to dream even bigger than we could on our own.

So that was the first meeting. And, once again, being the new kid in town, I really didn't know a lot of people at my new school. I was in the marching band. That was life for me in high school. It gave me an opportunity to instantly meet new friends and have some sort of stability and purpose. If you weren't in the marching band, I probably didn't know you. Mark was not in the marching band that year (for other reasons you will soon read) and so it wasn't until he rejoined the band in our senior year of high school that we actually started getting to know each other.

I'm not going to go through the details of how we became lifelong friends and started down this amazing and blessed journey together. Mark can remember those details and fine points a whole lot better than I can. And he can most definitely write it in book form better than I ever would. I'm struggling writing this foreword to his book; I have no idea how I would write the whole thing. But I will tell you that I am so thankful for the friendship God gave us in those late high school years that are so delicate and important in a person's life. Mark's friendship was a gift to me that helped me walk along my own Hurt Road and grow in my faith and gave me the courage to try to chase after dreams I'm not sure I would have by myself.

They say that people never change. And I suppose there's some sort of truth in that. Mark Lee is still a lot like he was back in high school. A library book nerd *and* a cool kid that can rock the guitar. A class clown *and* a deep theological thinker. A regular, blue collar, down-home guy *and* a man with a great realization of what's going on in the world.

I've always said that Mark is everyone's best friend. I've never met a person who didn't like him. He has such a unique sense of humor and is a personality that is truly one-of-a-kind. There's hardly a time when he leaves the room and people aren't saying, "That Mark Lee dude—he's a character." I've seen him crack people up with a joke and the next minute have them in a deep discussion about the Bible, politics, or world affairs.

It's interesting to read a biography of someone you've known for most of your life. You think you know someone. You think you've heard every story and every joke and every thought that a person could possibly have—especially with the time and miles and experiences you've shared together. But there's something special about someone telling their story and writing it down. Something interesting in the way a person—especially a man, most of whom are usually unable to express to each other vocally the things they feel deep down in their "heart of hearts." And that's what I love so much about this book—that I've gotten to know, all over again, one of the closest friends I could ever possibly have in all of my life. Through his humor that is so unique and smart, his wisdom that only comes with pain and loss, and his heart that wants nothing more than to search and know God more—hopefully you can get a glimpse into a great friend with a great story that will inspire and encourage you through whatever Hurt Road you may be walking down.

Mac Powell

ACKNOWLEDGMENTS

I've read somewhere that it takes ten years to become a writer. I guess I'm a little slow on the uptake, because my journey has taken closer to fifteen years. And so many people have helped me along the way.

Barry Landis was the first person to ever say "You should write a book," so he's the first I'm going to acknowledge.

To all of my team at Revell: I am forever grateful. Andrea Doering, thank you for your guidance, wisdom, and care. Twila Bennett, thank you for your ideas, hard work, and dedication. Lindsey Spoolstra, thank you for your attention to detail. Brittany Miller, thank you for all your efforts in getting the word out.

This book would not exist without the patient guidance of Kathy Helmers. Thank you for your optimistic reading of those early versions of this book. Thanks for showing me the difference between writing my memoir and my "memory scrapbook," and thank you for going to bat for me.

Thanks to all my mentors through the years: Steve Winter, David Wilson, Jeff Stone, Steve Rabun, Pete Hixson, Monroe Jones, Blaine Barcus, Terry Hemmings, and Jeff Gregg. Thanks to Randy Elrod for all the coffee and conversation at

Merridee's. Thanks to John Poitevent for the words of wisdom, the texts, and the encouragement. And massive thanks to Nigel James, Third Day's tour pastor, for shepherding us through the years and for sharing my love of classic rock, sports, and Marmite.

A huge thanks is in order to all my brothers in Third Day, past and present. Mac, you are my spiritual brother—thanks for starting this music thing with me. Thanks also for contributing the book's foreword. David, thank you for your heart, your integrity, and all those late-night talks on the bus. Thanks to Tai for your brains, and Brad for showing us how to rock. Thanks to Billy for being a great friend and mentor in the early days. Thanks to Scotty—your love of God, music, and other people is contagious. Thanks to Tim, Trevor, Brian, Geof, and Jason, for doing life together on the road. Thanks to our amazing crew—especially Brian Willis—for always taking such great care of us.

Thanks to my manager, Lott Shudde—you are probably Third Day's biggest fan and definitely the kindest person I know. I always look forward to our phone conversations. Thanks also to Coran Capshaw for your leadership and JP Durant for your hard work.

Thanks to Lillian Williams, my business manager. It has been such an amazing journey working together for twenty years. Your vision, your love for Third Day, and your enthusiasm are priceless.

Dan Raines—you offered such amazing leadership early in Third Day's career. What a blessing it is to have you on my team again. Jeanie Kaserman—thank you for your wise counsel.

Thanks to Keith Jennings. I am a better writer for all our chats about Brian Eno and *duende* and for our many years of bouncing ideas off each other. Thanks to Annie Downs for answering all my goofy questions. Thanks to Jeff Goins for helping me find my way in the early stages. Thanks to Becky Kraegel for teaching me about writing memoir.

Major thanks to Ben Pearson for the incredible cover photo. What an honor it was to work together again.

Thanks to my family at Stonebridge Church: David Eldridge for helping me find my "deal," David Scott and Penny Harrison for loving my kids, and my small group for all your prayers and support.

Thanks to all my family and friends through the years. You might not be mentioned by name in the book, but you were a vital part of my story. You supported, encouraged, and made me the man I am today.

Thanks to Tommy and Gail Turner for your love and support. And to think—I haven't even had to go on *Jeopardy!* yet. Maybe one day.

Thanks to Mom for taking off your "mom" hat and donning your English teacher one. I know this story was hard for you to read in places, but the book is better because of it. Thanks also to you, Stephanie, David, Jimmy, and Tammy for helping me sort through a mountain of pictures.

Biggest thanks of all to Stephanie, Abbie, and Kitty. I am the luckiest man on the planet having y'all in my life. You have generously sacrificed time with Daddy so I could work on this book. Thanks for your patience and understanding, but most of all thanks for your inspiration. You are the reason I want to write all these things down!

Lastly, I humbly acknowledge the Christian writers who paved the way for me: C. S. Lewis, Madeleine L'Engle, Max Lucado, Frederick Buechner, Richard Foster, John O'Donohue, and Brennan Manning. Thank you for your influence and inspiration. I am forever changed because of your writing.

1

ON THE ROAD

All right, let's bring it home. If you was hit by a truck and you was lying out there in that gutter dying, and you had time to sing one song. Huh? One song that people would remember before you're dirt. One song that would let God know how you felt about your time here on Earth. One song that would sum you up. You tellin' me that's the song you'd sing?

Sam Phillips, *Walk the Line*

I've heard people say that sometimes your brain will shut down just before traumatic experiences and you won't remember anything that happened. That may be true, but it surely wasn't the case for me. I remember every detail.

I looked up and saw headlights. There was no time to react. The truck was moving too fast.

I remember my body's impact with the front of it. Swept and thrown upward, I bounced off the top of the truck like a rag doll and spun up in the air. The streetlight above took over as the focus of my vision that the truck's headlights had been before. This light turned in circles in the morning darkness. For a moment I felt nothing. I was completely separated from earth.

Then I hit asphalt.

Adrenaline is a funny thing. I didn't feel myself making contact with the road so much as I was simply aware of it, like I wasn't living this myself but only watching it happen to somebody else. Because of that, I don't know exactly what part of me hit the road, but later the pain and lacerations on my face and right arm would let me know that these areas had absorbed the main force of the impact.

"Hey! Stop!" somebody yelled as the truck sailed through the intersection of Hurt Road and Powder Springs Road. The driver slammed his brakes, screeching the truck to a halt.

Wait a minute, I thought to myself. *I'm still alive. Aren't you supposed to die if you get hit by a truck?*

Emboldened by the adrenaline racing through me and numbed by the shock of the accident, I decided to attempt standing up. But my right leg refused to cooperate. I slumped back to the ground in the middle of the road.

I heard footsteps. A man from the nearby Quick Thrift gas station ventured into the middle of the intersection and knelt down beside me.

"Are you OK? Say something!"

"I'm OK. I think my leg is bleeding."

He looked down at my leg. "Yeah, your leg looks a little banged up. Help is on the way." He was trying to put a positive spin on the situation, but I could tell from his face that he was looking at something gruesome.

I began to shiver. Even though it still gets pretty warm in Georgia in October, the mornings can be pretty chilly.

I was supposed to be going to school for band practice. We were scheduled to perform in a big marching competition that night, and I had really looked forward to it. My plans for today had obviously changed.

I don't know how long it took—it seemed like a couple of minutes and an eternity at the same time—but paramedics were soon on the scene. Sirens filled the air, and the bright lights of an ambulance flickered and bounced off the side of the Quick Thrift. Two guys in uniform hopped out of the ambulance.

My name is Mark. And I'm on the road.

One came running up to me, while his partner stayed behind to prepare a stretcher.

Even though I was still in shock, I figured an attempt at comedy might be in order. "You guys want to buy some doughnuts?"

The paramedic tending to me chuckled. Then it was all business. "Hey, buddy, are you OK? Can you tell me your name and where you are?" Routine questions in accident situations.

"My name is Mark," I said. "And I'm on the road."

●●●

I've spent most of my adult life on the road. With my bandmates in Third Day, a rock group we started in high school that is still making music twenty-five years later, I have traveled pretty much everywhere—basically anywhere people will have us—and put on shows. Our lead singer and I used to be flat-out amazed whenever we traveled somewhere

23

new. We would announce it to each other. "Dude—we're in Illinois!" "Dude—we're in New Mexico!" I think we stopped doing that after about the third lap around the country.

As I write this the road has taken us to Iowa, where we are getting ready to do a little rock show. Later we'll do a soundcheck and an autograph session. Much later we'll perform. But for now I'm sitting on the bus watching a documentary about Genesis—the band, not the book. When I'm home I'm not much of a TV watcher. Between shuttling kids to activities and errands and home responsibilities I just don't have the time. But when we're out doing shows it's a great way to fill these huge swaths of time we find ourselves with.

Being a musician, I find some of my favorite shows are these rock documentaries where they give you all the nitty gritty behind-the-scenes details of a band's career. The series *Behind the Music* is a perennial favorite, but these shows have been made in some form or fashion for decades.

When I first discovered *Behind the Music*, I was mesmerized. I watched one on Tom Petty and the Heartbreakers and was amazed at how they started out happy-go-lucky, a group of friends making music together. Then they got successful and had to deal with some internal conflicts and some drug problems. But now the band is in the best place they've ever been.

Then I watched the Fleetwood Mac episode. It was even better. The band started out happy-go-lucky. Just a group of friends making music together. Then they got successful and had to deal with some internal conflicts and some drug problems. But now the band is in the best place they've ever been.

24

Or take the Aerosmith episode. A few friends got together and made some music, and then they got famous and it got really hard to handle the success. They got into drugs and they started fighting.

Living the dream

But then they learned to appreciate each other and the life that the band gave them. Now they're in a better place than ever.

Wait a minute. All these stories are exactly the same.

As much as I love *Behind the Music*, the stories all run together after a while because the show follows a formula. As with so many other things, we want to watch music documentaries and see a reflection of ourselves. These kinds of shows are doing what we all do every day of our lives.

How many times, when asked how we're doing, do we reply by framing our life like the end of a *Behind the Music* episode? Life is the best it's ever been. We had a rough patch, but now we're better than ever. Or at the very least, no matter what's going on, we tell people we're OK.

Inside us, something else is going on. "OK" is a form of wishful thinking. Even if we don't really feel fine, we want to. There's always a plan and a hope. *If I can get through this rough patch then I'm going to hit smooth sailing, and everything is going to be OK.* But it just doesn't work that way. All of us are trying to get to a place where everything's worked out and everything's easy. We're on the road to happily ever after, aren't we?

In *The Road Less Traveled*, M. Scott Peck says the core problem faced by modern-day humans is that we expect life to be easy. And like my bandmates and me being blown away the first time we went to Nebraska, we are flat-out amazed when life's not easy. But we don't chalk it up to the fact that maybe life is harder than we thought. Instead of learning from it, we look for someone or something to blame.

When I look back on my life, I can see that it didn't work like an episode of *Behind the Music*—and still doesn't. Try as I might, it's definitely not happily ever after. Good things happen and bad things happen. Sometimes they're happening at the same time.

It has never been easy. I have been dealt some rough blows. Accidents, injuries, losing a parent to cancer. While your road hasn't been the same, I'm sure it's had tough stretches as well. The road we're on includes sickness, job loss, tragedy, and death.

Even when we get where we're trying to go, it's rarely what we thought it would be. Surprisingly, success can be a trial in itself. The whirlwind created when we get busy doing something we love can make for a rocky journey that's tough to navigate. But while the terrain might be unfamiliar, the tools we use to navigate life are the same.

Each of us has a unique story, but together we're all on Hurt Road. We make our plans for how our lives are going to go forward, and the next thing we know we're landing in a ditch we didn't see coming. But we get up and we keep moving. The beauty comes because we're not walking alone. We can help each other and we can support each other. And, coming or going, God's got us. I have to keep learning this truth over and over, each time I start thinking again that I can walk my own road with my own plans. These are the landmarks that help me live freely, knowing that there is no right road or wrong road in life. We don't really get to choose that anyway—we just get to trust God, coming and going.

2

ONCE UPON A TIME

Life sort of comes at you and you come at it, and you
don't know what to make of each other.

John O'Donohue

We agonize over so many little decisions we're faced
with every day, even though so much was already
decided for us before we were even born. All those decisions
about when and where you would live and who you would
grow up with are pretty much set in motion by the time you
even enter the story.

Remember those horrible geometry proofs we had to do
in high school? We had to start with what was given to us.
Life is kind of that way. We all have givens, things we can't
change. And for me, that included Powder Springs Road, the
main drag that went through the area I grew up in, about
thirty minutes outside Atlanta. That road represents my

childhood and also the path I was on before high school and Hurt Road. It was my road to this idea of happily ever after.

For my first six years we lived in a neighborhood called Hollydale. Hollydale is near Marietta in Cobb County, one of the larger suburbs of Atlanta. As I grew up, Atlanta grew beside me in big, sprawling leaps. When I was born, the interstate wasn't even done in Atlanta. By the time I finished college, Atlanta hosted the Olympics. Cobb County is now the home

Jimmy holding newborn me

of the Atlanta Braves. I like to think we grew up together.

One time, when I was about six years old, I was riding in the car with my dad, driving by a long stretch of Georgia pine trees along Powder Springs Road. My dad pointed out the window at the rows and rows of pines we were zooming past and said, "Son, pretty soon none of these trees will be here."

At the time I thought my dad was crazy. But in my lifetime I've watched it happen. Atlanta, the fastest sprawling city in the history of the world (it's true—look it up!) grew out to our little lazy country suburb and swallowed it up without batting an eye. That grove of trees became a trendy shopping plaza. Then, as that area fell out of favor, it became home to pawnshops and import car repair places. I think a lot of those buildings are pretty well abandoned now. So much for home.

One of my earliest memories was getting a shot. I squirmed and cried. Through the pain I vividly remember the doctor saying I would need another one in ten years. For the next ten years I would sometimes think about it while I was waiting to drift off to sleep and I would get nervous. Then, after the doughnut incident, when I was in the waiting area, they gave me the shot. Didn't even tell me they were going to do it. Ow. Oh, that wasn't too bad. Every time that's happened to me, it's hurt a little less.

That's how it is when you're young. All experiences are first-time experiences. As poet John O'Donohue has said, life sort of comes at you and you come at it, and you don't know what to make of each other. As you get older and experience things for the second, third, umpteenth time, you learn all these little ways to cope with difficult things life throws at you. But when you're experiencing something for the first time, you don't have any coping mechanisms. You just kind of roll with it.

This was the 1970s, mind you, so all of my earliest memories involve a lot of shag carpet and big TVs. And all the men had even bigger sideburns. My parents didn't smoke, but it seemed like everybody else did. I'm pretty sure I wouldn't have made it as a grown-up in the '70s. Smoke makes me cough. And, try as I might, I can't for the life of me grow sideburns. But for a kid, it was a great place to be.

It was an era before playgroups and structured activities were the norm. Instead, kids were just sort of turned loose in the woods for hours on end because it was deemed good for us. It was the golden era of Saturday morning cartoons, and breakfast consisted of cereal—the more sugary, the better.

Hollydale was one of about a bazillion developments that sprung up around Atlanta in the late '60s. There was really nothing special about it, but we sure were proud of the name. I lived in Hollydale subdivision, went to Hollydale Elementary School, and, to round it off, attended Hollydale Methodist Church.

It was a great little community. All of the houses in Hollydale had these cool gaslights in their front yards. I remember how they would glow in the summertime when we'd play whiffle ball until dark, and the lightning bugs came out and competed with the gaslights for our attention. We'd forget all about our whiffle ball game and chase the lightning bugs until our parents called us inside to eat frozen pizza and watch *Little House on the Prairie*.

● ● ●

My mom was an English teacher and later a school librarian. She taught for a few years before my older brother, Jimmy, was born, then took a few years off to be with Jimmy and me while we were little. I have some really good memories of being at home with Mom and my brother. Always the teacher, Mom taught us how to read at an extremely early age. I think I was about three. From that point forward, if you saw me, I was lugging a book around. I am still that way.

Besides fostering our minds, Mom tried to instill in us a sense of adventure. One time Mom took Jimmy and me to see a house that was on fire. We were playing in our room and Mom came to the door. "Boys! Y'all come on. There's a house on fire down the street."

We walked down the hill, rounded a corner, and saw a commotion. There were fire trucks in a driveway. At the end of

30

the driveway, amid the pine trees, was a house. It looked a lot like our house, except there was a hole in the roof. Through the hole, every now and again, a tongue of fire came lapping out, like a snake sensing its surroundings. It was as if it knew I was there. I grabbed on to Mom's leg. It was terrifying and the coolest thing I'd ever seen, all at the same time.

Mom was from Elberton, a rural town not far from Athens, Georgia. Her father, my granddaddy, was a key figure in all of our lives. He had a cow pasture behind his house. He ran a little country store, and I have many fond memories of helping him with the cash register or playing in the woods with my cousins behind the store. I would go to church with him and proudly sing songs like "Trust and Obey."

Granddaddy served as a reminder of a simpler time and a simpler faith. Work hard. Love your family. Trust and obey.

● ● ●

While I probably had more in common with my mom, my dad was my hero. Dad was from Savannah and had served in the military for several years. He had been a drill sergeant, so he was loud. But he had this big, magnetic personality. And he was funny. All of the neighborhood kids loved him. He would be burning leaves in the front yard—it seems like people were always burning things in the '70s—and kids would come running up, and he would pick at them, and they loved it.

I wanted to be just like my dad.

By the time I was on the scene, Dad worked on planes at Lockheed during the week and served in the National Guard on the weekends. He would often talk to me and Jimmy like we were recruits.

"Boys, we need to get up tomorrow at oh-six-hundred hours." I'd go to bed fired up, thinking I'd get like six hundred hours of sleep. Then I'd be loudly awakened at 6:00 a.m. with a new understanding of military time.

One sunny Saturday Dad pulled our brown Chevrolet Impala out into the street to wash it. He got out the soap bucket and scrubbed it down, and then began to rinse it with the garden hose. Not wanting to miss out, I pulled out my fire engine push toy and drove it to the curb. I needed to get my car washed too. My parents displayed that picture proudly in the family photo album.

Dad's Army enlistment photo

While I distinctly remember that one without any help, there was another memory I only have because it was in the family photos. Apparently, one time during this era, I put on Dad's cowboy boots and walked into the living room to show my parents how awesome I looked. They agreed that I looked awesome, to the point that they took a picture and proudly displayed it in the album.

What's wrong with this picture, you might ask? Well, the problem was, those boots were the only thing I was wearing. So, for years and years, whenever a friend of mine—and later, a girlfriend of mine—came over and we looked at pictures, that little PG-13 moment from my childhood would get relived.

Dad was an excellent wheeler and dealer. One of his favorite things was to set up a booth at a local flea market and

Helping Dad wash the car—and all our toys too!

sell things. He was so good at it that the church put him in charge of the annual flea market fund-raiser. One Saturday I was bent all out of shape because I couldn't find my red fire engine. That afternoon Mom took me by the church flea market. In a row of Big Wheels and other toys donated by church members, I saw it. But before I could get to it and claim what was rightfully mine, another little boy came up and sat in it.

"Danny, it's perfect! It's just your size," came the voice of the kid's mom behind me.

"I'll sell it to you for a dollar," Dad piped in.

33

"We'll take it."

So before I even knew what was going on, my favorite toy had been sold. Such is the life of the flea market peddler's son, I suppose. I'm going to have to ask my mom about that one. While I'm at it, I'm also going to ask her if my dad really had a friend with a farm who took our dog when we didn't play with it anymore, or if they were just taking our dog to the pound.

Before Dad worked at Lockheed he had a variety of jobs, including driving a bakery truck for Little Debbie. We had an endless supply of Little Debbies at our house—probably a big factor in Dad being such a big hit with the neighborhood kids.

Dad loved spending time with my brother and me. He would take us for long hikes at Cheatham Hill, breaking off bits of bamboo as we walked. When we got home, he would whittle them into "dog whistles" for us. He would take us fishing off the bridge on John Ward Road. We never caught a thing, to my knowledge. Come to think of it, I'm not sure we even had any bait. But that's the kind of dad he was. It was about the fishing, not about what we caught. And ultimately it was about being together.

Once I tried to be an Olympic diver and jumped off a stack of milk crates in the backyard. Dad took me to the hospital. I got hurt a lot as a kid, so maybe the ER was old hat by then, or maybe it was a school night and my mom

Dad taking us fishing

34

stayed home with my brother, who knows. But that time my dad took me.

The last time I'd been there for stitches, I squirmed and cried on the doctor's table. This time it was different. Something about having my dad with me provided this calming presence, and I just sat there on the edge of the table while the doctor did whatever he had to do. (On a side note, I'm totally calling out those doctors because they told me they put some kind of "numbing" solution on it. I would bet money that it was water. But I digress.)

I remember, clear as day, walking through the parking lot of that hospital and getting in the car. It was later in the evening—the sun hadn't quite gone down, but it was pretty close.

We got in the car and started the drive home. As the car wound through the hospital parking lot, Dad looked over at me and said, "You were real brave in there, son."

I had tried so hard to be brave, to be some kind of hero, and it landed me in the emergency room. But I guess it worked, because Dad said I was brave.

● ● ●

My newfound bravery must have been fresh on my mind when Jimmy and I started swimming lessons that summer. Our church did the lessons sort of as a community outreach. They were held at a nearby backyard pool. The first day I was giddy with excitement, and I wasn't the only one. As we walked around to the back of the house I could hear the screams of delight from a bunch of kids who were already in the pool.

Swimming lessons the previous year had been a breeze. Mrs. Lowry had taught the littlest kids. She wore this green bathing suit and let us hold on to her while she swam around the pool. I loved it. I was a little scared of the water at first, but by the end of the week I was waving at my brother and the other big kids as we'd whisk by. This swimming thing was easy. Afterward we would go to the Quick Thrift and get Slush Puppies. I always got the cherry kind. It was so cold in your mouth but you couldn't stop eating it and then you'd get brain freeze. So good.

So this year I couldn't wait to show off my skills. Mom took our towels and things and found a seat with the other parents. While the instructors were waiting for everyone to arrive they let us get in the water and play. Giddy with excitement, I ran down the stairs and into the water. I made my way through the group of other kids, looking for a familiar face. In doing so I noticed that the pool had a slope on the bottom of the shallow end.

I just started walking down the slope. I was so proud that I knew this pool and knew what I was doing. Being the four-year-old that I was, I had yet to receive the memo about the whole shallow end/deep end issue when it comes to swimming pools. So I kept on walking. I didn't notice that the water was getting deeper, although I was vaguely aware that the cool Spanish mosaic tile on the side of the pool was rising and was about to be over my head. Then I heard a little clinking sound in my ears.

I was underwater.

Not sensing any danger, I kept walking. The pool must've had a steep drop-off, because I was very quickly at the bottom of the deep end. Far from being scared, I was fascinated. This world under the water was so unlike anything I had ever seen. The sun shone down into the pool in little pointy columns. Sound and light blurred together, and everything

was bubbly and echoing. I could hear the other kids screaming and playing but it was all muffled. Through the shim-
mery blur I could see in the distance some bright flowery
bathing suits as the other kids continued to play in the
shallow end. They had no idea how awesome it was in the
deep end.

It was the greatest minute or so of my young life. And
then the terror set in. I realized that I couldn't breathe and
I couldn't swim. I cried out and heard myself through this
gurgling wall of water. The pool was claiming me. At that
age you just sort of accept things as they come to you, so
this sudden fear was even more pronounced. I was going to
drown and there was absolutely nothing I could do about it.

It's hard to explain, but through the terror I began to sense
that someone else was there with me. Like the Hebrew children in the fiery furnace, there was the presence of comfort
and belonging there in that pool with me. And it was beyond
feeling or emotion; I knew it was a person. This person let
me know that it was going to be OK.

After what felt like forever but was probably just a few
seconds, I heard a splash and then felt arms around me. Another kid was now in the water with me, struggling to pull
me to the surface. It was Terri, one of the bigger kids. She
had seen me in the deep end, jumped in the water, grabbed
me, and was now carrying me back up the same slope I had
ventured down a few moments ago.

A few seconds later I was safely on the side of the pool
with Mom as a group of stunned grown-ups tried to figure
out what had just happened.

While I had many accidents growing up, this brush with
death would leave me asking that most human of questions

long after it was over: Why? Why did that happen to me? Why did I survive it? Did God have some reason in mind for keeping me around? I wouldn't begin to grasp these kinds of things until much later. But these questions were pointing me toward some bigger issues in life.

3

QUESTIONS OF FAITH

Questions . . . can make or unmake a life.
David Whyte, "Sometimes"

When you're really little, the world is a pretty stable place. The grown-ups are in charge and they seem to know what's going on. So you just kind of trust them and roll with it. As I grew up, I started asking questions. It was like noticing cracks in the world all around me. Hairline fractures, little imperfections that I first met with curiosity. As I began to notice more things, these cracks developed into something else. As much as the grown-ups tried to shelter me and protect me, I still caught the occasional glimpse of something big and scary lurking out there. And I began to doubt and question.

I saw bad things happening in the world. Mom watched the news every night, and when I came in from playing in the yard I'd watch it with her. Hostages were being held in Iran, dominating the headlines for over a year. Closer to home, children were going missing in Atlanta. It seemed like these events were all the newscasters ever talked about, and they terrified me. Why would God let these things happen?

One morning, as Jimmy and I were waiting for the school bus, Dad's car started to pull out of the driveway as he headed for work. He stopped and rolled down the window.

"Boys, John Lennon was killed last night," he said.

I didn't know who John Lennon was, but it made me very sad.

These cracks in the wider world soon spilled over into an area I thought I'd never have to question: my faith.

Church was a big focal point for my family. Hollydale Methodist didn't sport a steeple like other churches. It was built in a kind of modern fashion in the shape of a big triangle so that in a sense the whole church was the steeple. The inside had a bunch of wood paneling, and instead of pews we had plastic orange chairs like you'd find in a school classroom. There wasn't a parking lot when I was little. They just had this gravel driveway that extended around the church property and people would park somewhere along the driveway.

It wasn't a big church by any stretch. About a hundred people would show up on Easter and everybody would high-five each other. My family went every time the doors were open. I have many fond memories of helping Mom hold the hymnbook while we sang

Mom, Jimmy, and me

40

songs like "O, For a Thousand Tongues to Sing" and "A Mighty Fortress Is Our God."

I loved church. On Sunday mornings we would do this big assembly thing before Sunday school started. We would sing songs like "Do Lord" and "I've Got the Joy, Joy, Joy, Joy Down in My Heart." I thought the line was "Down in my heart Tuesday." I never did get what the significance of Tuesday was. Then they would give out pins for Sunday school attendance. We would get a pin if we went to church for a month in a row, and every month after that. Then you would get a one-year pin, then a two-year pin. I think I got up to the two-year level, then they quit doing the pins. My Sunday school attendance might have waned a little bit after that, but I can't be sure.

I asked a lot of questions in Sunday school. They were innocent enough. Where did the dinosaurs come from? Where did Adam's sons find their wives? But my bigger questions happened in "big church."

For a few fateful weeks in the early '80s, our pastor decided to try something a little different. The order of service always included prayer requests followed by a pastoral prayer. Then we'd all launch into the Lord's Prayer together. Then we'd stand up and sing the Doxology. This was a Methodist church, where great pride was taken in getting out of there at high noon and beating the Baptists to the line at the Bonanza. But the prayer request time kept getting longer and longer.

So our pastor came up with an idea. Why not combine the requests and the pastoral prayer? One Sunday he announced this new plan. He would start with a short prayer and then open the floor. People would then pray their prayer requests directly. I would sit there with my eyes closed. During the pauses I could hear the air-conditioning or the creaking of one of the orange chairs. It seemed to go off without a hitch, so we did it for a few weeks.

Someone would pray their prayer request directly, then the congregation would say in unison "Lord, hear our prayers." Unison is a big deal in Methodist circles.

Unbeknownst to me, one of the ladies in the church, who hadn't been there in a while and apparently had a bone to pick as well, decided that this new prayer format was her perfect opportunity. So one Sunday she came to church and sat near my brother and me down front. The service started, and then we got to the prayer time.

"Lord, I want to lift up my mom, who is going to the doctor for tests tomorrow."

"Lord, hear our prayers."

"Lord, I want to pray for my son, who's leaving for college this week."

"Lord, hear our prayers."

So far, so good. Breaking the law of prayer, I opened my eyes for a second and saw this lady who hadn't been around the church in a while. She didn't have her eyes closed either. I kind of looked at her sheepishly, but she glared and then looked away. I thought she was glaring because I had my eyes open (not taking into account that if she could see me then her eyes were open too).

She opened her mouth to speak. Was she about to get on to me in the middle of the prayer?

To my surprise, the lady began praying out loud instead. Well, I guess you could call it praying. She hurled out a litany of problems she had with the church—how they didn't support her, how she didn't like the pastor.

Of course, I was nine, so most of the details of her diatribe were lost on me, but I'll never forget how she ended it: "I hate you all." Then, as she walked out and passed another lady, she added under her breath, "Especially you."

There was a long silence. I kept my eyes closed. I heard the air-conditioning again. Her footsteps echoed through the place as she walked to the back of the church and out the door, which then closed with a clank.

Then, in a broken voice, from the front of the church, the pastor said, "Lord, hear our prayers."

What?

This incident just pointed out a lot of other things I'd begun noticing among the grown-ups. I would see the ushers up at the front, helping lead the service. Then I'd see many of them standing outside the front door after the service, smoking cigarettes. I'd hear the pastor talk about how God is love and we're supposed to love one another with that same kind of love. Then I'd hear many people in the church say bad things about each other.

I was looking at what these people were doing and seeing how it didn't line up with what they were saying. What I didn't realize was that we're all broken and in need of a Savior. More importantly, I didn't realize I was broken and in need of a Savior.

My first real crisis of faith, though, came not from a question I asked but one that was asked of me. When I was in elementary school my family moved from our Hollydale subdivision to a house on some land in Powder Springs. It was only a few miles away but it meant going to a new school, and we didn't have any near neighbors my age. It was a big adjustment.

Not long after our move I was spending the night with my new best friend at this new school. We had so much in common—he was a smart kid like me and could watch college football for days. We would climb trees together and see who could jump from the highest branch.

My friend also introduced me to a couple of things that blew my mind. The first would be the Michael Jackson *Thriller* album. Now, statistically, every household in America has a copy of this record. But we all at some point experienced this album for the first time, and mine was at my childhood friend's house. We played it on his parents' hi-fi stereo system, got out all the liner notes, and read along with MJ's lyrics. I was mesmerized.

The other thing he introduced me to was the world of recording. We used to amuse ourselves by recording fake commercials on his boombox. Much later this would blossom into my writing and recording my own music.

That night his parents were extra chatty with me. I guess I had spent a lot of time with my friend, because I now recognize this as his parents wanting to know this kid their son was fraternizing with. You know, making sure I wasn't some kind of elementary school link on the heroin distribution network. The parents were asking where we had lived before our move last year.

"We lived in Hollydale," I said. "Everything was called Hollydale. Hollydale School, Hollydale Church, Hollydale—"

My friend cut me off. "Wait. You go to church?"

This question cut me to the core. Remember, this was the '80s in the South. *Everybody* went to church. I had kind of been under the impression that it wasn't optional. You could choose where you went, but you had to go. Even suggesting that my friend did not go to church was like saying he didn't believe in America.

His parents tried to be diplomatic. "We've decided to raise

our son in a secular environment. We'll let him decide about religion later."

I didn't know how to respond. I felt like I had befriended that little Damien kid from that movie *The Omen*. That night I wouldn't have been surprised if they had busted out the snakes and started doing some devil worshiping.

I didn't like that they had used the word *religion*. To this day I have never met anybody who has used the term *religion* or *religious* in a way that hasn't bugged me.

Later that evening we were driving home from a pizza place and passed a church. My buddy looked at me like I was a leper or a pushy salesman. "You go to church? Why?"

I did go to church, but that second question was something I was still trying to figure out.

It struck me then that this wasn't just about church. It was also about God, about faith. Church had always been sort of a given for me, and I didn't realize there was more I needed to decide about.

I looked around and saw this broken world and had a lot of questions.

Why do bad things happen?

That lady at church had a point too.

God, do you really hear our prayers?

And finally, my friend had me asking the biggest question of all. Is faith in God all about whether or not you go to church? Or is it about something more than that?

These were way bigger questions than dinosaurs. Questions only God could handle.

● ● ●

I carried all those questions around with me for several months, vaguely aware I was missing something important.

I would catch glimpses every now and again that pointed toward a desire to make my faith in God complete. I remember visiting a church with friends around that time and filling out the visitor survey card. One of the questions was "Are you a Christian?" I thought that since I was going to a Christian church that meant I was a Christian, so I checked the "yes" box, but then I felt an ever-so-slight bit of guilt for having done so. Later I would hear relatives talk about "getting saved" or "accepting Jesus as my Savior" and wonder what that even meant. I was confused—I had thought that going to church made you a Christian. Obviously there was more to it than that. I wanted to figure it out.

Then, that summer, my uncle Terry had a powerful encounter with God. He had struggled for years with alcohol. Being so into music, I had always been impressed by his huge record collection. Impressed and a bit terrified. Whenever we'd go to his house, my cousins would show me which of the records we could play backward to hear evil messages. While we'd be at his house I thought it was the coolest thing. Then we'd go home and I wouldn't be able to sleep.

The change all started with my cousin Josh. A local church had a bus ministry that went door to door and invited kids to come to Sunday school. My cousins started going and loved it. Then Josh pleaded with his dad to go to church. As a dad now myself, I can say with confidence it's hard to say no to a child.

So Uncle Terry went to church. And he had a dramatic encounter with God. And like he did with the jailer in the book of Acts, God turned his whole life around in such a way that it spread out to his whole family—and I became part of the story.

Word got around to the rest of the family that Uncle Terry had been saved. Honestly, my first question was "Saved from what?"

Kind of in the same way that when I announced to my parents a few years later that I was "going with" a girl in my class in middle school, their response was "Where are you going?"

It all came to a head for me that Thanksgiving. My mom's sister, Aunt Annette, hosted a big family gathering in Elberton. We always called her "Aunt Nette" for short. She still makes the best macaroni and cheese on the planet.

After dinner, I was upstairs playing video games with my cousins. It was 1982, so the Atari 2600 was all the rage. I think they had just come out with Frogger for Atari. As I was trying to make my frog jump from log to log, Terry's oldest son, Terrell, was watching and waiting his turn. Knowing that they had all had this conversion experience and also knowing that I needed to make some kind of decision, I began asking some of my questions. What does it mean to get saved? Why do I need to "become a Christian" if I already go to church?

My cousin Terrell was older, probably in high school by this time, so we younger cousins looked up to him. He had recently become a Christian and was excited to share about it. I don't remember much else of what we talked about, but I remember he wanted to be sure I knew what being saved meant. He explained a few things about knowing that you're a sinner and that because you're a sinner you need a Savior. And he talked about the confidence he had that if a tree fell on the house and he died, he knew he'd be with Jesus.

My next questions were more practical. How could a tree fall on the house? Did there have to be a storm? Or could the tree just fall out of the blue?

Terrell thought this was the funniest thing. Then he got serious. "Mark, do you want to get saved tonight?"

I knew that I did. He put down his joystick, and my cousin Beth ran and got a Bible out of her room. They showed me a couple of Bible verses. One especially stuck out for me: "If you declare with your mouth, 'Jesus is Lord,' and believe in your heart that God raised him from the dead, you will be saved" (Rom. 10:9).

Then we prayed—Terrell and I, along with Beth and a couple other cousins. I remember Terrell telling me to pray from the bottom of my heart, so I reached down deep and prayed from that place. I could feel hot tears coming down my face and a feeling of warmth and light washing over me.

I don't necessarily think you have to act or feel a certain way to be saved, but you do have to feel certain. God meets people right where they are. In my case, he met me while I was playing video games on Thanksgiving.

I love that I'm a small part of my uncle Terry's testimony. I love that when it's all said and done and we're all hanging out in eternity, he's one of the first guys I'm going to high-five. I also love that I got saved on Thanksgiving. Every year when Thanksgiving rolls around, I have something of eternal significance to be thankful for.

After we prayed, my cousin suggested that we go tell my whole family about it. We went downstairs to the dining room, where the grown-ups were sitting around the table talking. He told them I had prayed and asked Jesus into my heart. But for some reason I was embarrassed. I think it's because I wasn't quite ready to go public with it. That would happen a couple years later, in sixth grade, when I had the opportunity to go through my church's confirmation class. In the Methodist tradition, confirmation is a time to take your faith public and to have other believers lay hands on you and pray for you to receive the Holy Spirit.

For me, personally, it felt exactly like what it sounds like. I knew I was already a Christian, but this confirmed it. I took my faith public and got baptized in the process.

The way my church did confirmation was that we would go to a class with the pastor for a couple of months. During this time we learned some church doctrine and history. Steve, our pastor at the time, was downright hilarious. Many of his sermon stories revolved around baseball, so Steve was OK in my book.

Through confirmation class, I learned that not only were all of those questions I'd been carrying around OK but God wanted us to have them. It was a sign of a growing faith.

After about a month of classes, the church had a big confirmation service. I wore a suit to church, and along with several other kids my age went down to the front and was asked some simple questions. "Do you confess Jesus Christ as Savior, and do you promise to serve him as your Lord?" I thought back to the prayer I'd said at Thanksgiving a couple of years ago.

"I do."

When it was time to be baptized, Steve reached his hand down into a bucket of water, scooped some out, and put his hand on my head while he prayed. I had that same feeling of warmth and light that I had at my cousins' house. John Wesley once had a powerful spiritual experience and said that his heart was "strangely warmed." I could totally relate.

Afterward I went and sat down with my friends and family. Somebody, either my brother or one of my friends, tried to pick at me about it.

"Did somebody get wet?"

I just smiled. I didn't care.

4

LANDMARKS

Set up signposts,
make landmarks;
Set your heart toward the highway,
The way in which you went.

Jeremiah 31:21 NKJV

Marietta, Georgia, is known for a lot of things. But it's probably best known for the Big Chicken. I know this, because the first thing people ask when I say I'm from there is "They still got that Big Chicken?"

In case you're wondering, the Big Chicken is a KFC built in the shape of, well, a big chicken. Big as in fifty-six feet tall. While I'm sure the food there is great—it's a KFC, after all—the Big Chicken is mainly known as a landmark, a way to give directions.

Even commercials on the radio will mention the Big Chicken when they explain locations: "Just two blocks south of the Big Chicken." Back in the 1990s, as part of a major renovation, they had to tear down the Big Chicken and completely rebuild it. For a few months we were all lost.

Just like we need landmarks to help us find our way around town, I'm pretty sure God has left us with landmarks to help us navigate our way through life. They're not answers written in black and white, because God has given us a say in the matter. They're more like clues to help us figure out the way and guides to help us get there.

Home is a landmark. Any navigational app worth its salt will show you how to get there. But home is just a starting point for most journeys. And when the destination is unknown, we need landmarks to help make our way. God also puts people in our lives to serve as landmarks. In those early days it was mainly my family, but there were also teachers and friends at school. And since church was such a big part

Me, in my element, with Dad

of my life, pastors and choir directors and Sunday school teachers would also prove to be very important.

Then there are those landmark experiences we all have. Some kind of strange alchemy happens in our brains, and for some reason we carry around certain memories with us more than others. Those memories shape us and help guide us as well.

I quickly found that faith itself was—and is—an important landmark in life. Prayer used to feel like a chore; now I found myself wanting to pray first thing in the morning. Soon after getting saved, I was given a picture Bible by some family friends and I tore through it, then started reading a regular Bible.

Faith is a definite landmark but it's just the beginning of the story. If life with God was only about faith, then God would just zap us up to heaven when we accept him into our hearts. He has something far more exciting than that. He wants us to have a part to play in his story.

A lot of people trip up on this idea and try to make it more complicated than it is. But if we look at how God wired each of us, what kinds of interests we have, we realize we have internal landmarks to point toward the reason we're here.

When we were really little, my brother and I had a Winnie the Pooh record player in our room. One of my very earliest memories was listening to a recording of "In the Hall of the Mountain King" on that record player. I loved to line up all my stuffed animals on the floor of our bedroom and do a concert for them, playing DJ and blasting records for them. We had some killer stuff too. "The Big Rock Candy Mountain." "Red River Valley." You know, the heavy stuff.

One day a couple of our neighbors came over, and we showed them our Winnie the Pooh record player. We put on

Glenn Campbell's "Rhinestone Cowboy" and cranked it to full volume, singing along, loud and proud. Somebody even donned a cowboy outfit. Probably me. Our parents heard the commotion and came in, and it turned into a full-blown concert.

One day not long after that, Dad came home from work and presented my brother and me with copies of Ace Frehley's "New York Groove" and Gene Simmons's "Radioactive," both on 45. We put this music on the Winnie the Pooh record player, and the scales fell from my eyes. My mind was officially blown. I wanted to play guitar just like Ace Frehley. While I didn't actually take any serious interest in guitar until much later, my mental wheels began to turn and things were set in motion for music to become my thing.

In hindsight it seems a little crazy that Dad would have bought us a KISS record at all. A few years later they were considered one of those evil metal bands we weren't allowed to listen to. But for a brief period in the late '70s KISS was a mainstream band geared toward kids. They had KISS comic books and collectors' cards, even a KISS Halloween movie. For a little bit there, all my friends seemed to have KISS posters on their wall and KISS records on their turntables. I guess Dad wanted to make sure we didn't miss out.

Part of the mind-blow was definitely the music itself. I was taken by the raw energy of this rock music. And I can't deny being drawn in by the aura of KISS: the elaborate makeup, the costumes, the carefully crafted personas, the fire. And let's not forget about the boots. But a big part of it was the fact that I was five years old and this was the music my dad presented me with. If he had come home with a polka album, maybe I would have wanted to play the accordion.

I think the fact that it was music was also very important. I'm sure there were other things that could have been important but they didn't grab me in the way music did. I remember one time my dad came home from a trip with the National Guard and presented my brother and me with pocketknives. My brother used his like you're supposed to. He probably still has it to this day. I took mine out and instantly cut my hand. My parents took the knife from me and told me I could have it back when I was "old enough." Apparently I'm still not old enough, because I haven't gotten that knife back—or any other. A couple of years ago, at a family Christmas function, we did one of those gift swap deals and I wound up with a pocketknife. I was genuinely excited about it. But everybody was concerned, and taking the knife from me at any available opportunity became the point of the game. So I guess it's a known thing that me and knives aren't a good combination.

It's also a known thing that I don't mix well with mechanical things with engines. When I was about eight or nine years old, we got a minibike, which is kind of like a motorcycle version of a go-kart. On my first chance I got to ride it, my dad and brother told me what to do to get the minibike to go. So I went. Before they told me how to stop it. Next thing I knew I had ridden the minibike across the street and into a mud bank. I was lucky I didn't get hurt.

So it's not just that Dad brought something home for me. It was something I was predisposed to like, I suppose. God wired me in such a way that I would like music and that I would like that particular kind of music.

Musicians often talk about influences, and my brother Jimmy would definitely go down as a major influence for me. From when I was a little kid, I would find many of my musical tastes in his record collection. He had both the *Grease* and *Saturday Night Fever* sound tracks, and *The Long Run* by The Eagles. I didn't know that I was supposed to hate those records. They were all part of the magic that music created for me.

Before school we would blast music in his room. Back then everything cool in Atlanta was offered up on a station called 96 Rock. We would listen to 96 Rock before school and get rocked by bands like Survivor and Foreigner, then we'd go to Turtle's to buy the records. If 96 Rock told us that an album was cool, Turtle's was the place to buy it. On the wall at Turtle's they had the Billboard chart, the same one Casey Kasem counted down every week. Later, when I got a radio of my own I would record the countdown, but for now I would just listen and write it down.

●　●　●

My mom began working in the school library and would take books home for Jimmy and me to read. In the summers I fought the heat by lying on the floor in my room and reading in front of a box fan. The public library hosted a summer reading club where you would fill out a form listing all the books you'd read over the summer. One summer I read seventy-nine books. My brother, never to be outdone, read one hundred despite always being off on his bike (or minibike) somewhere.

The work of C. S. Lewis is a landmark for me. One night a cartoon version of *The Lion, the Witch and the Wardrobe* was on TV, and my family talked it up beforehand like it was the latest Charlie Brown special. Of course, by this time all the cool holidays were taken, and the children of America were expected to get fired up by "It's Arbor Day, Charlie Brown!" I just remember being instantly attracted to Lewis's story. It reminded me a little bit of *The Wizard of Oz* in that it started out in our world but then went to a magical place. I remember liking all the Narnian creatures, especially Mr. Tumnus, and being pretty terrified of the White Witch, who could turn all those creatures into stone. I had a Turkish delight fixation for years afterward, and would tell other kids how much I loved it, despite not getting a taste of it until I traveled to the UK at age fourteen.

The Hardy Boys were pretty big too, as were other childhood classic series like Danny Dunn and the Boxcar Children. But one book stood tall above all others. It was the book that made me fall in love with books. I was first exposed to this classic in the first grade, not as a traditional book but as a filmstrip.

Since Mom had just started working again, when school let out my brother and I would usually stick around for the afterschool program. Kids in this program ranged from kindergarten to fifth grade. Younger kids like me were thus exposed to a lot of things early, like big kid books (and bad words!). Usually my brother and I would go for an hour or so after school. It was pretty crazy how *Lord of the Flies* things can get in just an hour, but that's another story entirely. Usually we'd have a snack and then play a bit, building some kind of fort or another in the woods behind the school, and then we'd get picked up. They usually showed a video or a filmstrip at the end, but Jimmy and I were usually long gone by then.

But there was this one day where we were among the last kids there. It was winter and the weather was bad, so we didn't play outside that day. As I sat in that first-grade classroom with the Letter People on the wall and the desks pushed together in little islands, I remember thinking about how late it was. At that age you don't think about time and get frustrated. You just notice how things are different from the usual. And when you're young, you don't count time by clocks. My stomach told me all I needed to know. The cookie and chocolate milk snack they gave us right after school had long since worn off.

On this day they played a filmstrip called *A Wrinkle in Time*. I remember being absolutely mesmerized. The plot revolved around a girl who was struggling at school who met up with these three strange ladies who took her on all these crazy travels by "tessering" through time and space. The villain wasn't really a traditional "bad guy" at all but rather this foreboding dark cloud called The Black Thing. All of these elements made for a fantastic tale like nothing I'd seen before. Mom tracked down the book in the school library and I was hooked.

This was during the time my family was moving from our Hollydale house to Powder Springs, a more rural area of Cobb County, and I would have to change schools. Something about all the books I was reading, and *A Wrinkle in Time* in particular, acted as an anchor at a time when everything else seemed to be unraveling. I think the main thing that struck me about that book was how the magic was woven in with ordinary life in a way that made it feel real. Instead of having kids fall down a rabbit hole or walk through a wardrobe to find a fantasy world, the fantasy world coexisted with our own. Instead of the kids going to this other place, the other place came to them. At this point my life had begun to lose its magic. It was encouraging to know that maybe, just maybe, there was still a little bit of magic out there in the world.

5

WHEN CALLING COMES CALLING

And if the people find you can fiddle,
Why, fiddle you must, for all of your life.

Edgar Lee Masters, "Fiddler Jones"

Rick Warren's book *The Purpose-Driven Life* is a personal favorite of mine. It places the vast majority of its focus on the things that *all* of us are called to do as Christians and only a couple of short chapters on our individual callings. When Rick Warren does get around to what God wants each of us to do, specifically, he encourages his readers to just experiment and try a few things until something clicks.

My friend Keith Jennings has taken this idea a step further. He feels that none of us have an individual calling at all. Our calling is to go wherever God calls, whenever God calls, no matter the cost. We should stay open to God's prompting each and every day. I haven't thought this one all the way through, but I think Keith is on to something. It's a very freeing place to live from.

I think my pastor David Eldridge has landed on a great middle ground. He calls it "doing your deal." David believes that all of us have been wired the way we are for a reason. God wants to use each of us through our own unique gifts to reach those around us.

Is it a calling? Is it a ministry? Perhaps, but that's beside the point. And that's why I like David's "deal" idea. Instead of placing the idea of purpose on a pedestal and making it this all-important decision we have to figure out, we knock it down to the realm of the everyday. Which is exactly where I believe God wants us to focus.

But what are those gifts? If we all have a calling or a purpose or a deal, where in the world do we find it?

Most of the landmarks pointing to our purpose can be found in childhood.

It's funny how many of the biggest decisions of my life happened almost automatically. I am a musician, so I would love to think that my first decision to take up an instrument involved prayer, fasting, and fanfare. Or at least a second thought. It didn't.

One day after school, when I was six years old, I was playing with a fishing pole in the driveway of our house in Hollydale. Dad had set up a plastic plug on the end of a pole so I could practice my casting. I threw out the line as far as I could, then saw Mom's brown Chevy bump over the curb and into the driveway. She got out of the car with a question for me. "Mark, would you like to take violin lessons with Mrs. Protteau?"

"OK."

It is absolutely crazy to think how many other major decisions in my life have been of that nature. I'd like to think that my odds at success have probably been about the same as anyone else's but I've saved myself the hassle and worry of weighing the pros and cons of a major decision. In this case, it was the decision to become a musician.

That night we loaded the family up and drove down Hurt Road to Austell Road to Ken Stanton Music. Upon entering the store I was filled with that wide-eyed wonderment of experiencing something for the first time. I was immediately taken by the smell of wood. Hanging on the walls were all kinds of strange-looking brass and wooden musical instruments. I recognized the guitars and the trumpets and the flutes, but there were so many more. I wanted to learn about all of them.

A salesclerk with red hair and a mustache presently walked up to us. "How can I help you?"

My mom answered, "This is our son Mark. He's about to take violin lessons, and we wanted to see about renting him an instrument."

The word *rent* stuck out to me. Rent sounded too much like *borrow*. I wanted this violin to be my own.

"OK, let me show you what we've got."

"We should probably let you know that he's left-handed. Do you carry left-handed violins?"

"We do, but if I can offer you one piece of advice, it would be to start him out on a right-handed violin. I always recommend it because it's so much easier to find an instrument that way. And you have to use both hands anyway, right?"

My parents and the salesclerk shared that polite kind of laugh that grown-ups do. But because of that, I grew up playing violin right-handed. Later, when I took up guitar, I would play it right-handed as well. Sometimes I wonder if I would've been some kind of virtuoso had we not taken the advice of that red-haired music store guy.

The drive home felt like it took hours. I just couldn't wait to get home and play my new violin. When we did finally get home, I ran to my room and took the violin out of its case. I arranged all my stuffed animals in rows on the carpet in front of the bunk beds, just like when I'd play them songs on the Winnie the Pooh record player. But this time, instead of being the DJ, I was part of the band. I proceeded to give them a full-on concert. The fact that I had no idea how to play violin didn't matter one bit. I dragged the bow across the strings and they let out a satisfying screech.

Before the Grammys, before the Doves, there was the cafetorium at Hollydale Elementary School.

My mom's vision for me involved playing classical violin. For the next ten years I would take violin lessons and eventually played in the school orchestra. My dad, on the other hand, dreamed of me playing country fiddle. I have many memories of him calling me into the living room to see some guy playing fiddle on *Hee Haw* or *Austin City Limits*. On this night, however, I was living out a dream of my own. I was Ace Frehley from KISS, and my stuffed animals were the good people of Detroit who came out to get their faces rocked off. And it was my duty to make their ears bleed.

● ● ●

Christmas at the Lee house usually went something like this: we'd get up ridiculously early and open our presents. This first part was no big deal. My brother and I would jump out of bed in the wee hours and happily tear into our presents. One year we got Star Wars toys. Jimmy got Luke Skywalker and an X-wing fighter. I, on the other hand, got the bad guys: Darth Vader and the Death Star. I loved them.

After opening presents each year, Dad would ask the same question.

"OK, boys. You got your bags together? Let's go."

Then we'd load into the family station wagon and make the five-hour drive to Savannah.

Dad was from Savannah and his family was big. He had six brothers and sisters, and his brother Larry threw a big Christmas party every year. The whole thing was chaotic, starting with our piling into the station wagon and taking off. Almost everything was closed on Christmas in those days, so we could pretty much count on at least one meal at a Waffle House along the way.

That one Christmas when every child in America got Star Wars toys

We'd roll into Savannah, and I'd be thrust into the world of Dad's family. His mom, my grandma Allie Fae, was always joking and always speaking her mind in a loud monotone.

One year she got a new microwave. "The directions said to put potatoes in there for two minutes. I knew potatoes take forever so I put them in there for thirty minutes. You think that's all right?"

"Did y'all go to church this morning? 'Cause you know you got to go to church on Christmas and Easter to show the Lord whose side you're on."

I still use that one to this day.

J. D. Lee, my granddaddy, looked just like my dad but older. He might have been the nicest guy in the world but he couldn't hear anything. I was always too intimidated to talk to him because you had to raise your voice to just about screaming pitch to be heard, and I never got up the nerve to do that. Granddaddy Lee worked on diesel engines and always gave us cool Mack Truck hats when we'd come to visit.

My dad's brothers and sisters all loved to carry on just like Dad did, and because it was such a big family, the food was gone instantly whenever it came time to eat.

Despite the chaos, Christmas in Savannah always ended up being fun. There was food and presents, and Jimmy and

Hanging at Granddaddy's store, the centerpiece of so many great childhood memories

I would end up running around in the woods building forts with our cousins. Savannah was noticeably warmer than Atlanta, so you could do that kind of thing even in December. But I always dreaded it because I was so shy and I didn't know them very well. And the big, boisterous crowd that always turned up at Uncle Larry's didn't help matters.

Uncle Larry wasn't a musician himself, but he collected musical instruments. Hanging on his wall were guitars, banjos, and fiddles.

My cousin Jason was my brother Jimmy's age and was a big music fan too. One of my favorite things to do at Christmas was hang out with my cousins in Jason's room and listen to his records. Later on, I'd learn about bands like Extreme, the Kentucky Headhunters, and even Zac Brown from my cousin. This year, though, I think he had just discovered the Fat Boys. So about seven or eight of us were crammed in Jason's room learning about the glory of old school hip-hop. Of course, back then it wasn't old school. It was just plain awesome.

The noise must have reminded the grown-ups that we were in there, because Dad stuck his head in Jason's room. "Son, why don't you come here a second?" he asked me. "I got something to show you."

I followed Dad and Uncle Larry to the wall with all the musical instruments. Uncle Larry had glasses like my Dad, and the two of them resembled each other quite a bit. If it were possible, Larry might've been a little crazier than my dad too.

"Your daddy says you know some tunes on the fiddle. You want to try mine out?" He took it off the wall and held it up in front of me, along with a bow.

Christmas at Uncle Larry's

I looked at the fiddle. The violin I played was quarter-size, made specifically for kids. My teacher had attached little pieces of tape to show me where to put my fingers. Uncle Larry's fiddle was full-size and it didn't have any tape. I gulped.

Dad must've told Uncle Larry I might say no, because my uncle was prepared. "OK, how about the mandolin? It's tuned just like a fiddle," he said, grinning. "It's just got four extra strings. Try it."

I had heard of a mandolin, but had never played one. I wasn't expected to know how to play this strange instrument, so it didn't come with any added pressure in the way Uncle Larry's fiddle did. Curiosity won out over nerves, and I picked it up and plucked the strings one by one, *pizzicato* style. It did sound a lot like the violin I was used to.

I picked out something simple like "Twinkle, Twinkle Little Star." The feel of frets under my fingers was kind of strange, but other than that, it seemed easy enough.

Then Uncle Larry took back the mandolin and handed me the fiddle.

He looked at me and smiled. "Go on. Play something."

I put the fiddle on my shoulder and placed the bow across the strings. I didn't really know what to play, but they were looking at me, so I'd better play something.

Whatever kind of Jedi mind trick they had been trying on me was working. I loved how Uncle Larry kept calling the violin a fiddle. Maybe I should play a fiddle tune? I launched into a tentative version of "Turkey in the Straw." I started out sort of playing quietly to myself. The more I played, the braver I got. By the end of the song I was playing full volume.

One thing I should note about the violin. It is a loud instrument, so there's really no such thing as tentative.

Next thing I knew, a crowd of grown-ups was around me.

"Wow, Mark! That's great! What else do you know?" one of my aunts asked.

I launched into one of my other favorites, a lullaby by Brahms.

"Do you take just classical? Do you know any other songs?" one of my cousins asked. I guess they liked it.

Over the next twenty minutes or so, I played all the songs I could remember, from the classical stuff to the *Star Wars* theme to fiddle tunes like "Old Joe Clark." My family seemed genuinely delighted.

This was a totally new experience for me. Up to that point, I had looked at music as another chore. It was something I had to do, along with schoolwork and cleaning my room. And it was done alone, in my room. At best I would play for my parents to show them I'd been practicing. But after that night, I played my violin whenever I got the chance. I'd play hymns in church or *Star Wars* music for our neighbors. The joy that it brought other people never got old.

But Dad was always my biggest fan. When I was practicing at home I usually liked to tear through songs so I could move on to more important things like watching TV and playing basketball. But Dad wouldn't let me off the hook quite that easily.

"Play it right, just like you're playing in front of a real audience."

He was especially critical when I played hymns. They were held in a special regard, above any other songs, and he would encourage me to play them reverently, not skipping any of the verses.

● ● ●

I don't know how the whole finding your purpose thing works. I assume it's different for everybody. But for me, the word *calling* fits perfectly. I felt a strong pull toward music and truly believe that I was called into music the same way others are called into ministry.

When I was in sixth grade, my parents took me to see *Amadeus*. I was absolutely mesmerized. The film was a tad long, and I was of the age where a movie would pretty much lose me if it didn't make me laugh or at least offer some on-screen explosions. But fortunately, I was also at the perfect age to be enraptured by a movie about a musician.

The sound track really drew me in, especially the way the music unfolded, changing tone from lighthearted to down-right somber as Mozart's life drifted toward its end. Catching a glimpse of what a creative soul like Mozart might have been like was inspiring.

Later that night, I woke up with a start.

Music. I want to do music. This is what I'm supposed to do.

I had that same warm tingly feeling that I had the night I prayed from the bottom of my heart at my cousin's house. The same feeling I had when I got baptized.

I know what you're thinking. I got fired up watching a movie and decided I wanted to do the same thing. And if I hadn't followed through with it, if there had been no fruition, I would agree with you. But because I'm writing this over thirty years later, over twenty of which have been spent as a professional musician, I've got to think there's something to it.

After that I practiced with a new resolve. I guess I assumed I would play some kind of classical music. Actually, to be totally honest I hoped I would continue to play the violin, but I envisioned playing it in a rock band such as KISS. It never occurred to me how goofy, how impossible this dream would be to pull off. By the same token, had I stayed on this path I might've ended up like Boyd Tinsley from the Dave Matthews Band, or at least playing in a country band or something. But God had other plans.

Even though I was a massive rock music fan by this point, I did not really like the guitar. I always associated it with nerdy dudes with bushy hair and glasses playing folk music on PBS. (If you're a nerdy dude with glasses who has appeared on PBS playing folk guitar, my apologies. I'm sure you're awesome.) And after playing violin, the frets on the guitar always felt like cheating to me. So I just never bought into it. I played violin from the time I was six all the way through high school. If there is one thing I regret, it's that I didn't keep it up into adulthood.

My parents taught me that I'm supposed to finish what I start, although they never really did define "finish" in the case of playing the violin. I just kept at it, and kept expanding my musical outlets. In sixth grade they gave us the option of playing an instrument. Since our school didn't offer orchestra, I decided to play trombone in the band.

The summer in between seventh and eighth grade, my mom asked me if I wanted to play the piano. It's funny—I don't recall really wanting to play the piano. I had gotten a cool little Casio keyboard for Christmas a couple years prior, and I guess my mom thought I would like to learn how to play piano in earnest. She had learned about a teacher named Mrs. Cook who taught both violin and piano.

Mrs. Cook was exactly what I needed at that point in my life. Mrs. Cook took music seriously. Or maybe she took me seriously. Whatever it was, she pushed me and challenged me to really practice and really focus on technique, and this helped me get better. She had a knack for making it fun. But most of all, she had a belief in me that I don't think I had in myself yet. At the end of my eighth grade year, we did a concert at a local music store. Mrs. Cook gave out awards at the end, and I was named Student of the Year.

6

SUCKER PUNCH #1

I like to think that one day you'll be an old man like
me talkin' a young man's ear off explainin' to him how
you took the sourest lemon that life has to offer and
turned it into something resembling lemonade.

Dr. K. to Jack, *This Is Us*

Before my wedding day completely put the kibosh on
the idea of "happily ever after," it was a concept that
shaped me as I grew up, to the point that it would form the
backdrop for most of the early decisions I made.

It started with an innocent trip to the principal's office.

We used to have chicken-fried steak along with biscuits and
gravy at school quite a bit. As a kid growing up in the South
in the era before they started cracking down on unhealthy
lunch fare at school, this kind of thing was pretty common
for me. One particular day in seventh grade, the gravy was a
little on the thick side, and a couple other kids and I started

theorizing, asking that dangerous and powerful question "What if?" Now, some "what if" questions are so powerful, so advanced, that only thirteen-year-old minds can muster them up. We deduced that if you got just the right amount of gravy on the biscuit, and threw it at just the right angle, the biscuit might—just might—stick to the ceiling. But only a test would reveal the answer. I thought it was a cool idea, but I quickly tried to change the subject. I was kind of a goody-goody as a kid. Certainly not biscuit-throwing material. But then a dare was made, followed quickly by a double-dare. The next thing I knew, I had dipped the biscuit into the gravy and lofted it in the general direction of the ceiling.

Amazingly, it stuck! For a brief second I, along with my entire class, sat there flabbergasted, marveling at this impressive display of physics. I beamed proudly. But pride comes before a fall, and in this case it was a literal fall.

The biscuit fell back to earth, and along with the biscuit the wrath of my teacher rained down. I was promptly sent to the principal's office. The principal actually had a pretty good sense of humor about it, and my only punishment was that I had to go ask the custodian for cleaning supplies and then clean up the mess myself. This was probably a good idea, in theory, but at thirteen I had very little in the way of cleaning skills. Try as I might, all I was able to do was make a gravy-colored stain on the school's ceiling in the shape of a near-perfect circle. It remained there as long as I was at that school, reminding me of that ill-fated day. I like to think it's still there.

But something the principal said that day stuck with me. "You might get away with that stuff in middle school. But when you get to high school, you'd better look out. And one day, the Real World is going to hit you hard."

73

Toward the end of eighth grade, I got a similar lecture from a teacher. This one was all about how things were going to be tougher in high school. "They're just getting you ready for the Real World."

This made perfect sense to me. All of my life was leading up to a certain point in the future, which seemed to happen in the Real World. And I believed that when I reached that point, everything would fall into place. This idea centered around me getting through high school, getting into a decent college, landing a great job, and getting married. That was the goal; that was the road that led to happily ever after.

I'd had glimpses of it before that day in the principal's office. I'd be sitting in class the day before spring break and the clock would be ticking and time would feel like it had about stopped. Or I'd be waiting in line at Six Flags, just dying to ride the Scream Machine, and the line took forever. I would think if I could just get through this one thing, whether it be school or a long line, it would be smooth sailing.

It was beyond the idea of sacrifice and reward. Sometimes you have to work hard to be able to enjoy yourself. I had to practice the violin to get any better, even when *Space Giants* was on TV. Good grades only came through study and keeping up with homework.

This Real World idea my well-intentioned teacher was talking about, this was something different. It made me wonder. I mean, is childhood something you get through just so you can get to the part that counts? Was all my life up to that point like the wait in line for the roller coaster? That was my first glimpse of happily ever after. When I got through school, when I grew up, I'd enter the happily ever after of the Real World.

This idea may not have felt right at first, but it began to fit me the more I wore it. And as I looked around, it seemed like everybody was operating out of this happily ever after principle. Get through the week so you can enjoy the weekend. Get through the boring work part so you can go on vacation and have fun. *If I can just get through this, then everything is going to be OK.*

Starting in seventh grade, I looked forward to the happily ever after of high school. But when I got to high school, it was a lot tougher than I thought it would be. The classes were hard and it seemed like everybody but me had grown about a foot taller over the summer. Every day was just looking forward to the happily ever after of getting through it and going home.

Until one Saturday morning in October.

● ● ●

"Mark, get up. We're going to be late."

I managed to open one eye part of the way, squinting at my mom through the lone, piercing light. As I tried to piece my surroundings together, something just didn't add up. It was Saturday. Why get up so early?

"Late for what? I don't have to be at band practice till nine."

"Remember, you said you'd pitch in at the doughnut sale for MYF. You can help them for a while and then go to band, but we'll need to leave soon."

I lay there as long as I could get away with it. The night before I had been to a football game. My school marching band had performed at an away game, which meant I didn't get to bed until really late. Getting up early the next morning, on a Saturday, felt like a cruel joke.

Mom cracked the door open again.

75

"Come on, Mark. Get up. And you'd better grab a sweat-shirt—it's cold out."

I let out a sigh of defeat, then kicked the covers off the bed, put my feet on the floor, and reluctantly got ready. At the last second I remembered what Mom said. I couldn't do anything about selling doughnuts, but I could be a little less cold. I grabbed a hooded Georgia Tech sweatshirt and walked out to the driveway to find Mom waiting in the Caprice.

I was surprised to find out just how cold it was. And dark.

October weather in Georgia can be pretty indecisive. It still gets warm in the afternoons, but when the sun goes down it can be rather chilly. It was right before daylight savings time—at this early hour there was no sun out to help matters.

I had agreed to help sell doughnuts for my church youth group that morning because of sheer numbers. It was a really small group, so if I didn't show, attendance for the doughnut fund-raiser would be down by like 10 percent. So I went. Upon arriving at the church I was met by several other bleary-eyed teenagers and a handful of caffeinated grown-ups. We were split into groups of two. I was paired with a girl named Jennifer, and her dad drove us to the Quick Thrift down the street. We parked and set up shop, which involved opening up the back of his Blazer where the doughnuts were and waiting for customers.

We stood in the parking lot waiting and watching the traffic at the intersection of Powder Springs Road and Hurt Road. It was still dark. I guess we were working on some sort of plan, waiting for the light to change. I kind of zoned out, still tired from my short night of sleep and maybe a tad nervous about the prospect of selling doughnuts to strangers. I had never really been much of a salesman up to this point, even though Dad was well known for his propensity for wheeling and dealing. A few weeks prior I had "helped" Dad run his flea market booth. He put me in charge of it for about half an hour and I managed to lose twenty bucks.

The light turned red and a yellow Datsun pulled to a stop in front of us. I sprang into action. I walked out into the intersection, carefully watching for cars. In the car was a scruffy looking dude who looked like he'd be more at home on a motorcycle.

"You want to buy some doughnuts?" I tried to act confident, but the tremble in my voice said otherwise.

"Sure!"

Hey, this isn't too bad. Maybe I'll make a good salesman after all, I thought, not realizing that Krispy Kreme doughnuts pretty much sell themselves.

I took the money and handed the guy his doughnuts.

Smiling sheepishly in the general direction of Jennifer and her dad, I started to walk back to the curb. Maybe it was the excitement of the transaction or the early hour, but I failed to notice that the light had changed while I had been in the intersection.

"Hey, buddy, look out!"

Those four words, uttered by a total stranger, would split my life in two.

I looked up and saw the headlights, but there was no time to react. The next thing I knew, I was strewn across Hurt Road along with my money and my doughnuts.

I tried to get up, but my right leg felt all wrong. Unable to support my own weight, I slumped back to the asphalt and laid down.

I heard traffic going by. People who were in a hurry. They were on their way to places. Jennifer's dad knelt beside me and tried to make small talk.

I began to shiver. I was thankful Mom had reminded me to wear a sweatshirt. Later I would find out that the scruffy guy who bought the doughnuts had grabbed my hood and tried to pull me out of the way of the oncoming truck. Sometimes it's the little things that save you.

I would find out all these crazy details later, along with bizarre others. Like the fact that the guy driving the truck was named Mr. Coffee. Coffee and doughnuts. You just can't make these kinds of things up.

"Here are your doughnuts, man." The man in the car had picked up all the doughnuts that had been scattered in the incident and gave them to me, along with the $2.50 that I had apparently dropped when I was hit.

As we waited on help, I lay there in disbelief. I had been fairly accident-prone as a kid. Trips to the emergency room for stitches were a regular part of my childhood, but I had never spent the night in a hospital. I didn't know what was wrong with my leg, but I was pretty sure an ambulance had been called, and I would soon be whisked to a hospital. At this point in time, I felt so cold that I actually looked forward to going anywhere but here.

"Do you want to buy some doughnuts?" I asked the paramedics, when at last they arrived.

The paramedics chuckled. They were probably used to seeing all types in their line of work, and I'm sure some people in traumatic situations tried to use comedy as a coping device.

This would become my go-to line, not just with the paramedics but also with the X-ray technicians at the hospital, the doctors, the nurses, and anyone who came to visit.

I probably could have made a lot of money for the youth group if I actually had any doughnuts with me.

The comedy didn't end there. When I went back to school, I had to tool around campus on my crutches—tentatively at first, but I got better. People would pass me in the hall or under the big bell tower in the center of campus and they'd say "Hey! It's the Doughnut Man!"

"You got that right!" I'd yell back as I gave them a sarcastic thumbs-up.

While I was in the hospital, the rest of the trombone section at my high school paid me a visit. They presented me with a trombone that somebody ran over with a truck. "It's the Dumb Trombone Award!"

The paramedics on Hurt Road that morning probably didn't pick up on my sarcasm. How could they? They didn't know me from Adam. But beneath the comedy was anger. And fear.

I had absolutely no idea what was going to happen. A few minutes ago I had been just trying to sell doughnuts for a little while and then get to marching band practice. Now I was wondering if I would ever be able to walk again, let alone march in the band.

I don't remember it, but at some point I was placed on a stretcher, then loaded up in an ambulance. Despite my multiple trips to the emergency room, I'd never ridden in an ambulance before. We began to move, and they turned on the sirens. This wouldn't take very long. The intersection where we were selling the doughnuts was only about two miles from the hospital, and they had just built the first segment of a new four-lane connector road.

I would also later learn that after dropping me off at church, my mom had gone to the grocery store. The ambulance passed by the grocery store on the way to the hospital and Mom heard the siren. She even thought about me and the other kids selling doughnuts and hoped everyone was OK.

I was extremely tired. Lying on this stretcher, I felt my lack of sleep catch up with me, along with the sheer exhaustion of the ordeal I'd already been through.

"You think it would it be OK if I slept a little?" I asked.

"No, buddy. If you fall asleep you might not wake up."

I laughed nervously. I think he was half-kidding, but when you're half-kidding, you're also half-serious. I figured I'd err on the side of serious, seeing as how I wanted to live to tell the tale of my first ambulance ride.

We got to the hospital and they unloaded my stretcher and wheeled me in. I was taken back to some kind of holding area. Finally, after all these times I'd had to wait at the emergency room, I thought they were putting me through to the front of the line. Nope.

They put this cool temporary cast thing on my leg and then took me into a room to wait. And wait.

My dad was the first person I remember seeing at the hospital. I tried the "Do you want to buy some doughnuts?" line on him. He laughed and told me that, if nothing else, this would all make a great story someday. My youth leaders were soon there, as well as Mom and Jimmy. I'm sure some of the other kids from youth group tried to be there too but ended up hanging out in the waiting area.

They did some X-rays, then took me back to that same holding room. They did some more X-rays, then took me back again. I met the doctor who was going to be doing the surgery. Apparently I wasn't going to lose my leg, but I had broken both bones below the knee. The doctor called it a "ski slope fracture," which apparently was something pretty severe. Bottom line: it was going to be a long road to getting back to where I was.

That first night in the hospital, Mom brought me a boombox and some cassettes. She even bought me the latest R.E.M. album. And she played it pretty well too.

"Mark, your favorite band is REO Speedwagon, right? I got their new cassette for you."

"Come on, Mom. I told you it was R.E.M."

Mom smiled. "Good. Because that's what I got you."

That night, after one of the nurses came to check on me, I had a hard time getting back to sleep. I remembered the boombox. I turned it on so low that I couldn't hear it at first. But then my ears got used to it and I could hear it. It almost sounded too loud. In my darkened hospital room, I played that R.E.M. cassette from start to finish. When that was done, I flipped it over to the radio. The new song from Aerosmith, one of my favorite bands, was playing.

Music was there to hang on to, like a lifeline, like a landmark. God gave me music as a "big thing," a calling and purpose. But he also gave it to me to help navigate through the day to day. When I didn't know where to turn, the landmark was there.

Somewhere during this time, the initial shock of getting hit by a truck wore off, and the truth began to set in. Things were never going to be the same.

7

IF I CAN JUST GET OVER THIS

After each failure . . . pick yourself up, and try again.
Very often what God first helps us towards is not the
virtue itself but just this power of always trying again.

C. S. Lewis

One of the craziest things about getting hit by that truck
was my first reaction: I tried to get back up. In a big picture sense, that's also what I tried to do with my life. Before
the truck incident, my road to happily ever after consisted of
getting good grades, getting into college, and getting a job
after I graduated. For the next several months I wasn't on
that road anymore. I'm not even sure I was on a road at all.
Instead I found myself in a ditch trying to figure out what
in the world had just happened.

I had surgery on my leg and then stayed in the hospital
for several days. I was visited by family and friends. My
goal during this time was simply to get home. Once I made

it back home, my existence became lying on the couch and watching TV. It was cool for a while, as I watched just about every James Bond film ever made.

But then boredom set in. My friends got busy with school activities and I found myself alone for much of the time. I missed several weeks of school, only going a few days between my accident in October and Christmas break.

On the few days I was at school, I would learn that it's easy for people to help with what's on the inside when it's been knocked to the outside. People are a lot more likely to help you carry your burdens when they're easy to see. I was the kid on the crutches—the Doughnut Man. And people were happy to help. People would open doors for me and other kids (girls!) would help carry my books. It was a nice surprise.

One day during this time, I figured that since I was on crutches I'd just skip out on communion at church. God would understand. But one of the ushers did the coolest thing. Right at the beginning of communion, as Pastor Steve was breaking the bread and getting ready to pray over it, the usher knelt down beside me.

"Son, would you like to take communion this morning? We can bring it to you right here."

I didn't know what to say, so I just nodded my head. Next thing I knew, Steve came down and broke me off a piece of the communion bread and handed me a glass of the grape juice. He then prayed over me, just like he would for the whole congregation.

It was a nice gesture, and the kind of thing I saw quite a bit during that time.

But after a while, I just wanted to get back to normal. The problem was I didn't really know what that meant anymore.

Happily ever after had been knocked out of me and I had been rattled to the core. But the idea didn't go away completely. It just sort of morphed into something else. My goal at that time, my happily ever after, became just getting back to the path I'd been on. I never would admit it, but I kind of missed school.

It was hard to keep up with my studies when I was absent so many days from school. The school sent a homebound teacher who came once a week and offered tutoring. This actually helped quite a bit. Most of my teachers were understanding, and most of my grades didn't slip.

Except for typing class. We had a typewriter at home, and I did my best to keep up, but it was hard to do everything required for that class. I really hoped the teacher would be forgiving.

She wasn't.

I got a C in typing. As funny as this sounds, that was a big moment for me—a big turning point for the worse. You know how when you're playing a video game and you die and you know you're not going to get a high score so you just hit the reset button instead? That's pretty much what happened for me at that point. My happily ever after was now just getting back to normal, and making the honor roll wasn't really a part of it.

Unlike the apostle Paul, whose faith was unwavering while he was blown off course, mine faltered a little. I never doubted, never "lost my religion" as Michael Stipe would talk about a couple years later. But faith in God lost its prominence in my life. It wasn't an intentional thing. It just took a backseat to everything else. It was like a slow fade at the end of a song, just a little less each second. I was busy and struggling to keep up with school, on top of the typical stupid teenage things like worries about being cool, impressing friends, or spending probably too much time with one girlfriend or another.

But most of all I think I was jaded. After the initial shock of my accident, I was surrounded by friends and family. Then most of them left, and every morning when I woke up I was quickly reminded of all the things I couldn't do. Even as my body tried to recover from the accident, I was in a general funk spiritually. I felt numb.

Numb is hard ground for faith to grow.

People would pray for me when they saw I was hurt. I would always nod in agreement, but I didn't feel anything in my heart.

● ● ●

A few weeks after I got home from the hospital the first time, I went to a new doctor who said that my leg wasn't set right and that he was going to suggest another surgery. The upshot was he gave me the go-ahead to go to one of our high school's football games in the meantime. I guess my leg couldn't get any worse.

This was a big deal for me. McEachern High School had—and still has—one of the biggest stadiums in the state. Think Friday Night Lights before they had Friday Night Lights. The stadium regularly hosted marching band competitions because it was tall enough that you could watch a band march and actually see what was going on.

We were called the Indians, and at one end of the stadium a big statue of an Indian chief overlooked the proceedings. He held his hand up as if to salute the other Indians on the field. Or maybe he was saying goodbye to the other team, I'm not totally sure.

Of course, what I wanted to do at the game was sit with my friends. My friends were in the marching band and, as you can imagine, the marching band got the best seats in the house. I'm kidding, of course—they were thirty or forty steep rows up in the dizzying heights of the massive concrete stadium.

At this point, other than doctor's office visits, a few sporadic days at school, and a couple trips to the grocery store, I really didn't have any experience walking on crutches. Especially not on stadium bleachers. A couple of my friends tried to help me make the ascent, but by the time we got about halfway up it was obvious I hadn't thought this through. At one point my precarious grip on the guardrail gave way and I started to fall. I braced myself in the only way I had left—by stepping on my broken leg. When I stepped, I used all the muscles that you take for granted when walking, and they did great. But beside that, I felt things crunching together that weren't ever meant to be together.

This was a bad idea.

I somehow managed to get to a seat. I didn't even get to the trombone section on the top row of the stadium—I was so freaked out that I happily sat on the front row of the band with the flute players. Even now, all these years later, I can hear our exciting conversation.

"How you flute players doing? Thanks for letting me sit with you."

"It's not 'flute player.' It's flutist. And it's not pronounced 'flutist,' it's pronounced 'floutist.'"

I had a riveting time. Honestly, I can't remember much about the game. I just remember being so nervous about how I was going to get back down those steep stadium steps. My fourteen-year-old mind pictured a fire truck pulling up to the side of the stadium with a really long ladder. Or maybe they could call in a helicopter to airlift me out. Either way, I would never live this down.

But then I saw, walking up the steps, none other than Steve, my pastor. I guess my parents had told him about my predicament, or maybe he just saw me up there and figured I needed help, but I was so relieved.

Steve calmly walked up to my perch. When he got to me, he took on the tone of a baseball manager having a meeting at the mound with a flustered pitcher.

"The way I see it, we've got a couple of options. Somebody could carry you down, but I'm pretty sure that's not going to happen. Or I could just stay one step in front of you. If you start to go down, I'm pretty sure I'll break your fall."

So that's how we did it. He would take a step and then I would hobble down after him. He would take another, getting two stadium steps ahead, then I would hobble down one more.

Step. Hobble. It wasn't pretty but it was efficient. And before I knew it I was down at field level. Believe me—I was totally fine with watching the rest of the game from down there.

This was the first of many times I realized that if I was going to get through this, it was only going to be with a lot of help—like Steve letting me lean on him on those stadium steps. I was going to be OK if I remembered I had all these people around me I could lean on.

And when it became apparent that I was going to be out of school for a long time, I started spending a lot of time with my dad.

● ● ●

In the months after my run-in with the truck, I would be in the hospital, then home again, then back to school for a few days. Then in the hospital again, then home again. During this time, Dad changed shifts at work so he could be home with me during the day. Before I got hit by the truck, my primary activity had been playing basketball. After the accident, this turned into sitting in front of the television most of the time.

This was at the height of MTV's heyday. I would watch MTV for hours. Pop metal bands like Bon Jovi, Cinderella, and Poison dominated the airwaves, as did college music like U2 and R.E.M. Even though I was supposed to like one type of music and make fun of all the rest, I gravitated to all of it.

My dad was doing some watching of his own. I suppose he saw my interest in music and my background playing violin and decided I could play guitar. I had never really been that interested in guitar, but his excitement must have rubbed off on me. On my fifteenth birthday he took me down to Dirt Cheep Music and bought me a guitar. I wish I could tell you that it was some old Martin or at least a Gibson and that I still have it and play it to this day. I wish I could tell you I even still have it. But it was a piece of junk, and I don't remember how much it cost. I don't even really remember getting it. I just remember playing it in the store.

The dude strummed a chord and that guitar sounded great. In hindsight, I wish he had strummed another chord, because I later found out that the guitar was horribly intonated and would not hold tune for multiple chords. But you could tune it up to play one shiny, strummy G chord and it would sound great. That's how he sold me on it.

Less than an hour later I was holed up in my room, sitting on the green carpet next to a treasure box I had made while I was in Cub Scouts. I had popped the cassingle of Cheap Trick's "The Flame" into my boombox and was now trying to figure out how to play it. I didn't know a single thing about guitar, but I figured I'd dive right in and figure it out.

Dad's hunch about me playing guitar would prove to be spot-on. From this point forward, I was in full-tilt guitar mode. I taught myself a couple of chords and even bugged a friend who played guitar by calling him and getting him to tell me how to play chords. He'd put the phone up to his amp and play Guns 'n' Roses songs, then try to explain how to pull it off. For some reason the songs just didn't have the same conviction when played on my out-of-tune acoustic. I didn't really learn much, but I had a blast trying.

That summer I saved up my money and bought an electric guitar from a friend. It was literally a pawnshop special. And by literally, I mean he forgot to mention the small detail that we had to go to the pawnshop and get it out of hock before I could buy it from him. At some point I'm sure it crossed my mind that I could've just bought the guitar from the pawnshop. But I guess I was being nice.

I thought a lot during this time about my near-drowning experience all those years before. I guess one brush with death reminds you of others. Or maybe it was something a little more. Maybe this landmark memory was pointing to something that was going on. Just as there is a whole different world to be found in the waters of the pool's deep end, maybe there's a whole world of hurt we're all carrying around. Just below the surface of the deep end of life, maybe all of us are in need of rescue.

8

SUCKER PUNCH #2

Emily: Does anyone ever realize life while they live it
. . . every, every minute?
Stage Manager: No. Saints and poets maybe . . . they
do some.

Thornton Wilder, *Our Town*

The next fall after the accident, I went back to school
with a new resolve. I had lost the crutches and was even
cleared to join the marching band again. By the middle of
my sophomore year I had recovered reasonably well from
my injuries, and things seemed to be getting back to normal.

So maybe I had lowered the bar on happily ever after a little
bit. Coming off my run-in with the truck, I wanted to put
Hurt Road in the rearview mirror. I could just do the regular
high school routine for a while. My big life plans could wait.

Then we started noticing something was wrong with Dad.

In hindsight, there were signs, little hints just below the surface. Dad would laugh at things that weren't funny. He repeated himself a lot. It was enough to make me scratch my head but not enough to make me worry, at least at first.

I first got worried about it one day when we were out driving. It was a sunny afternoon right after school, and my spirits were high. I had recently gotten my learner's permit, and Dad was letting me drive around town. I usually enjoyed driving with Dad. He was laid-back and tried to make it fun. His driving advice was hilarious yet true: "Drive as if everybody else on the road is a complete idiot."

But Dad's mood was a little different that day. He seemed a little bit edgy, grumpy even. I thought it might be because of his new work schedule.

"Stop the car. Let me show you," he said.

I pulled over at the next corner. In front of us there was a big truck carrying mulch. Dad had us switch places. Was it because there was too much traffic? It was late in the afternoon and rush hour could get pretty crazy. I thought it a bit odd, but chalked it up to another of his offbeat teaching tactics.

He pushed his glasses against his face and squinted a bit in determination.

"OK, let's see. First you put your foot on the brake, then you put it in drive. Wait, that's not right."

He wasn't talking to me so much as mumbling to himself. A chill ran through me along with the realization of what was going on.

My dad wasn't showing me anything. He was reminding himself how to drive.

A couple weeks later I came home from school to find my dad asleep on the couch.

"Dad! You're late for work!"

He slowly got up, muttered something to himself, then went and got ready. A few minutes later he left.

I didn't think too much about it until later that night when the phone rang. It was my dad's work. He had never shown up, despite my seeing him get ready and leave.

I was terrified. I'm not sure what happened next, though I'm sure my mom called around to see where Dad was. I went to bed and pretended I was asleep.

About one o'clock in the morning, Dad walked through the back door.

"Where in the world have you been?" my mom asked.

"Ranger, North Carolina. I was sitting in a restaurant looking at a plate of spaghetti. Then I thought 'What am I doing here?' I remembered we live in Georgia."

I'm not sure if I slept that night. I was scared for sure. But I was mainly just mad. *Why me? Why now?*

Obviously something was wrong with Dad. A doctor's appointment was set for Monday morning. That weekend we tried to make the best of it, but Dad just wasn't himself. He kept saying things that didn't make any sense. I remember hoping that maybe it was something easy. Maybe Dad just had some kind of chemical thing in his brain. A guy at our church struggled with mental stuff, anxiety or something. His doctor put him on some medicine and now he was totally fine.

But in my heart I knew it was something major. I figured my dad either had something serious, like cancer, or had lost his mind. Either way, I knew things were never going to be the same.

On Monday, Mom took Dad to the doctor. Jimmy and I went to school like usual. When we got home nobody was there. Mom called a bit later to say they were heading to the hospital to run more tests. Then she called later that night.

"We're at the hospital. You need to come here right away."

Jimmy and I with Dad during his battle with cancer

"Mom, just tell me what it is. It's cancer or something, isn't it?"

"Just come up here."

Jimmy drove us to the hospital in silence. I think we both knew it was something serious. Otherwise Mom would have just told us. When we got there, she broke the news. "It's cancer. They're getting him ready for surgery now."

I was getting hit by the truck all over again.

● ● ●

You know how there's that good cry where you're trying to give a speech but you're about to lose it and you cry a little? People like those, because they see a little glimpse of reality. Then there's the bad cry, where the glimpse becomes full-view and it's just not pretty.

I often feel like if I ever just lay it out there, if I ever really say how I feel, it's just going to get awkward. It will be like the bad cry. People might even laugh at me.

93

People want us to be real, but not really.

Brene Brown says this so well in *Daring Greatly*, that what many women want is not so much for men to share their feelings but for men to lie about their feelings in a way that sounds real.

I think, since he was a guy and all, my dad probably felt pretty much the same way, which is why he never really told me he loved me when I was a little kid. He let me know I was loved, don't get me wrong. We'd be reading a story at bedtime or he'd listen to one of my records on the Winnie the Pooh record player with me. Then he'd say something like, "You know Dad loves you, don't you?"

I really would have been OK with that.

But something changed that night at the hospital. By the time I even knew my dad had cancer, they were getting him ready for surgery. Nobody really said anything, but the unspoken thing we were all thinking was that this was probably it. By the time I headed back home later that night, I was fully anticipating that my dad might not live another day.

Which is why I'm so glad he told me. I don't know how alert he was through the fog of the cancer, but I guess he knew it was serious and that he might not get another chance.

While we waited in Dad's hospital room, I just sat in silence for a good while. With all the chaos around me, it was pretty easy to just lie low. I was used to seeing people in the hospital. My brother had an extended stay with a bone infection when he was younger, and I had spent quite a bit of time there myself a little over a year ago. Sitting in this room, staring off into space, I think I was in shock. I didn't want to believe the news, even though I knew.

One of those little Southern pastoral phrases that gets tossed around is "your heart of hearts." As in "Do you know you've been saved? In your heart of hearts?" As if your regular heart wasn't enough but your heart had a heart too and you had to make sure that other heart was also in agreement.

Well, I knew in my heart of hearts that something was wrong with my dad, and at this point I knew in my heart of hearts that he might not make it.

I didn't say anything—what was there to say? After sitting for a while, I got ready to leave. Jimmy stayed behind and visited for a bit longer. I always felt like Jimmy knew Dad a little better, so he probably had more to talk about. The flip side is I think he might've taken it a little harder. But who's to know, because we all had that unspoken agreement that we all cared about each other.

But that all changed right before we left. Mom told me my dad wanted to talk to me. I went back into Dad's room. I could tell that something was weighing on him even more than the cancer.

"I love you, son," he said.

"I love you too, Dad."

I knew my whole life that my dad loved me. He had shown me in so many ways. He patiently sat through my football practices when he probably would rather be somewhere else—and let's face it, I probably would've been better off somewhere else. He played with me and my brother when we were little. He took me fishing and hiking. He was there for us. He had our backs.

But it meant everything in the world to hear him say it.

● ● ●

If finding out that Dad had cancer felt like getting hit by another truck, then the next several months of my life were like another pitiful attempt to stand up after being hit. Not only could I not get up but it felt like I was getting full on body-slammed back onto Hurt Road.

Dad ended up getting through the surgery OK. Those few days were so intense and I was so focused on my dad getting through the surgery that I hadn't even begun to process another difficult truth that lay behind it.

My dad had brain cancer.

I didn't even know what that really meant for him, for his future, or for our future as a family. I guess I thought they would do the surgery and then he would be better and everything would be back to how it was before. What ended up happening was that they did the surgery and got everything they could. Then they began a round of radiation treatments. Then they did another surgery. Then they added in some chemotherapy.

Because all of these procedures were being applied to his brain, his personality literally changed before our very eyes.

I guess Dad's personality had changed before the diagnosis, when he became forgetful and confused. Then, right after that first surgery, it changed again. Dad still couldn't remember things but now on top of that he started acting like an ornery old man.

A year or two prior I had gone to the UK on a school trip and bought one of those newsboy caps. Dad thought it was pretty hilarious and started wearing one too. This new post–cancer surgery incarnation of my father started wearing the hat again, but without an ounce of sarcasm. And he started carrying a cane around too.

A few days after the surgery I was driving with my parents, on the way from school or a church function or I forget what. I was about to turn onto our road. Dad was in the backseat and was angry about something. I don't know if it was my driving or that he wasn't driving, but he let me know about it.

"What are you doing?"

I rolled my eyes. "Trying to drive."

Now, I'm not sure if my dad picked up on the eyeroll from the rearview mirror or from my tone. My statement was most certainly uttered with some degree of teenage sarcasm. But the next thing I knew, the cane had moved from questionable fashion accessory to definite weapon. He swatted me in the back of the head a good two or three times before I was able to pull the car over to the side of the road. For just a second, my dad had been replaced by someone else.

We did our best to look past this kind of stuff because it was obvious that Dad was in a lot of pain. He couldn't sleep at night and had intense headaches that required he take a lot of medicine. Even if he had been in his right mind, I think he would have been out of his mind.

Later that spring, Dad went in for another surgery to relieve the pressure on his brain. As a result, his personality changed yet again.

This time, he became this combination of sweet old man and little kid. He laughed a lot and was able to see the humor in everything. He liked to count things. He liked going to places like Dairy Queen. The payoff for me was we went to Dairy Queen a lot. He was really nice but still really forgetful. He still didn't sleep much at night and would forget whether he had eaten or not. He had always liked milk but now consumed it by the gallon. As a result, Dad put on a lot of weight. The cane stayed, as did the hat, both now because of necessity. He couldn't really get around like he used to, and all of his hair had fallen out from the surgeries and the radiation.

Right before Dad received his initial diagnosis, some friends of mine invited me to go to a job fair at Six Flags Over Georgia.

Dad and I, circa 1982

I got a job in the games department. Looking back, I wonder why I didn't stop everything and realize that my dad was only going to be around a little bit longer. Why didn't I drink in every second? But I know that I had no idea how long we had. I guess I thought he was going to be around a long time. Now, when I look back, like Emily Webb in *Our Town*, I want to slow down and cherish every moment. But it didn't happen that way.

Even after Dad's first surgery, I kept my amusement park job. So my weeks were filled with school, and the weekends were consumed by my part-time job. And the most important thing in my life was that I wanted a car.

Fortunately for me, one of the most important things in my dad's life was getting me a car.

One thing he had going for him in this new personality thing was that he was focused. Usually on the nearest thing at hand. If we were parked in the Morrison's parking lot, he would say something like, "You know what I've always wanted? To eat at Morrison's." Even though everybody in the car knew he didn't like Morrison's, it wasn't worth the conversation. So we'd go in. Dad would get his food and say, "This is terrible! Who wanted to come to this place anyway?"

Dad got in his head that I needed to get a car, so in the weeks leading up to my birthday, every day after school was

spent looking at cars. To be fair, he had also taken me looking right before he was diagnosed with cancer. But our car
quest really intensified after he got sick.

One day we were out driving around and we passed by
a house that had a beautiful light-blue Camaro parked out
front with a sign that said "For Sale." I thought it looked
amazing and could already picture myself behind the wheel.
But I knew there was no way, so I kept it to myself.

"Let's stop and look at it," Dad said.

I was floored.

We took it for a test drive. I loved it. My mom threw out
that "I'm not sure but if it's OK with your father" kind of
vibe. But it seemed like my dad wanted to get it almost as
much as I did. So we gave them a little earnest money. Then
the next day we came back and picked it up.

There's an oft-quoted saying that starts, "If it seems too
good to be true . . ." I've never gotten that saying right because I think I'm on a perpetual quest to find something too
good to be true.

I would later learn that the good folks at Chevrolet made
a few different versions of the Camaro in the '80s. There
was the kind with the big, fast engine that you saw in all the
magazines. Yeah, I didn't have that kind. Mine was the one
that took the engine out of a Chevy Citation and put it in a
big sports car. So it looked cool but ran horribly.

At least once a month, something fairly major would go
wrong with this car. The upshot was I learned a lot about
cars in the process. I became an absolute expert at handling
a broken-down car. I learned that if you break down on the
side of the road, you should leave a note for the police that
you are coming back to retrieve it. Actually I kept one of
these notes in my glove box because I needed it so often.

So even though I had what I had thought was a cool car, it stayed in the shop more than I drove it. My car would be dubbed the Poky Little Puppy. I usually ended up driving my parents' station wagon, which we lovingly called the Woody Wagon. Because, as I'm sure you've guessed, it was that especially heinous version of the ubiquitous '80s station wagon with the fake wood paneling on the side.

The situation with my car infuriated me. I don't know why, but it made me mad at Dad. I guess because he had been as excited as I was. And he usually was really good with cars and mechanical stuff. If he weren't sick, wouldn't he have steered me away from buying a bad car?

There are so many things that happened that year that I feel bad about. Memories during this season carry a lot of pain with them. There are so many things I wish I had done differently. So many things I wish I had said.

On Dad's birthday, what ended up being his last birthday, I took him to get a birthday cake. With him so into Dairy Queen at this point, it only stood to reason that's where we'd get his cake. When the guy took the order, he asked what I wanted it to say. I had never ordered a cake before, not to mention the fact that I was a punk kid, so I just shrugged my shoulders.

"Whatever you guys normally put on it, I guess."

As we were leaving, Dad was upset. "Why didn't you say 'Happy Birthday, Dad,' when they asked you?"

I didn't have a good answer for him. I still don't.

Another time I drove to guitar lessons and Dad rode with me. I was new to the whole driving thing, not to mention that I was—and still am to this day—horrible in parking lots. I found a spot that was close to the building, albeit three stores over from the music store.

"You're embarrassed of your old dad, aren't you?" he said.

I really wasn't. I really just did a bad job parking. But even now, I carry that one around with me too. I wasn't embarrassed. He was my dad, no matter what. Why didn't I speak up and tell him that when I had a chance?

Summer turned into fall, and I started a new school year. I didn't do marching band that year. In fact, if you look at my high school yearbook, I did absolutely zero outside activities save the Latin Club. I didn't have any kind of new excitement or plan of attack regarding this new year. My goal was now simply survival. I just wanted to get through it.

Things were kind of in a holding pattern with Dad too. He still had to go to the doctor all the time, and would do another round of chemo and some more radiation before too long. One day my mom asked the doctor what he thought my dad's prognosis was at this point, and he said that he couldn't say how long anybody would live. He implied that Dad was in a pretty good place, and he was. Dad was still confused much of the time, and would never be the way he had been before that first surgery, but he was stable.

We actually got into a pretty good groove. Life was uneventful for the most part. Dad had even spent a week with his family in Savannah toward the end of the summer.

Maybe we didn't keep track of Dad's slow decline because we were so focused on the day-to-day. What is it they say about when it feels too good to be true?

That Christmas I remember sitting in the living room at my granddaddy's house in Elberton. Everybody was done eating and we were getting ready to do presents in the big room. It was just me and Granddaddy. I was flipping through the channels on the TV, looking for a ball game.

"He's fading fast," Granddaddy said. He didn't have to say anything else. Granddaddy was pretty opinionated and set in his ways, but he was perceptive for sure. And he would prove to be right.

Dad got to where he couldn't do much on his own. Fun was replaced with tired. He slept a lot. When he wasn't sleeping, he just kind of mumbled to himself and rarely interacted with the rest of us. Mom got worried that something might happen if he was alone too long, so I was recruited to come straight home from school and hang with Dad.

In February of my junior year we did some family photos. Jimmy, Dad, and I all wore jackets and ties. As we were sitting for the pictures, the photographer kept saying things like, "Keep your head up, Jim. Now smile. Just one time. Smile."

I don't know if anybody kept those pictures, but I hated them. Looking at those pictures for the first time was the point that I realized that Granddaddy was right, that Dad really was getting worse. He just looked sick and tired in those pictures. And the thing I hated about it most is that despite the photographer's pleading, he never did smile.

● ● ●

Over the next couple of months, Dad's slow fade turned into a rapid decline. One weekend in March, Granddaddy visited from Elberton and brought my cousin Beth with him. We had gone to eat barbecue earlier that night, and I'm pretty sure this was another case of Dad picking what was right in front of him.

"Why don't we ever go to Wallace's Barbecue?"

"Because you don't like it."

"Yeah I do. I love it. Always have. We should eat there tonight."

We all agreed to go, and even acted surprised when, after eating a few bites of his food, Dad scowled. "Whose idea was it to come here anyway?"

That night the family visited a bit and then went to bed with plans to get up and go to church together the next morning. Because of the extra company, I slept on the couch in the living room.

At about one or two o'clock in the morning, I was awakened by Dad's late-night wanderings. This had been pretty much a nightly occurrence for the better part of the last year, but lately it had been different. That night he was wheezing a lot. Walking, even the very act of breathing, came only with a great struggle. He was also mumbling to himself. When he made his way through the living room, I grabbed a pillow and folded it over my face, trying to go back to sleep.

BAM!

Dad had fallen—hard—in the hallway by the piano, just a few feet from where I was lying. It was a miracle that he hadn't hit the side of the piano and hurt himself worse. His breaths now came in short, labored gasps. I clenched the pillow over my face a little tighter, begging for this to be a dream. Throughout the house, lights came on and people sprang into action.

Granddaddy was first on the scene. "Jim! What happened? Are you OK?"

At this point, I knew I was in the clear, so I raised my head groggily and yelled "Dad!" in my best *ABC Afterschool Special* performance.

I still have a hard time thinking back on that moment. I wish I had risen to the occasion and tried to help. But being a teenager is so hard. You want, and are often expected, to be an adult in many situations. But a lot of times, especially when it's something hard to face, you still respond like a child. I used to be really hard on myself when I would think about this. Now that I'm a father with kids of my own, I give myself a lot more grace than I used to. I was just a kid.

Mom called the doctor, and it was decided that Dad was probably just in shock from the fall. The best course of action would be to wait until the next morning and take him to the ER.

I'm not sure if I slept much that night. I had suspected it for a while, but it felt like we were nearing the end.

That point was driven home further the next morning. We tried getting Dad out to the car—we even enlisted the help of a neighbor—but try as we might we could barely get him off the couch. It's one thing to help a grown man to a car—we had done that several times over the previous year. But a barely responsive, overweight cancer patient was another matter entirely.

So we called an ambulance. They were able to wheel a stretcher into our den and somehow got him loaded up. And so it was that on this crisp, early spring morning, a little over a year after Dad had been diagnosed with cancer, he would leave home for the last time.

Watching the ambulance turn around and exit our drive-way, I thought back to my own ambulance experience a little over two years ago. That seemed so long ago and so mild compared to this. There might have been a second, maybe right when I saw the headlights of the truck, that I felt my life was in danger. After that, even at my lowest, I knew that I was going to be some level of OK. Whereas I had a brief run-in with death and a long road to recovery, Dad's experience involved a long, slow march to the inevitable.

They put Dad in the hospital again. In the middle of all this, I tried as best as I could to maintain that all-important sense of normal. I signed up to work at Six Flags again, even applying for a foreman position. During that interview, I didn't say anything like, "Oh, by the way, my dad has cancer and he's not doing too good. So be ready because one of these days I might need a couple days off."

Besides the amusement park job, I also started working at the local public library. Since Mom worked at the library at the middle school, she was part of that clandestine librarians' network, passing along secrets from one library to another. I think the top-secret information was stored on those weird microfiche things. At any rate, she found out about the job at the public library.

I went in for an interview. Because I was of noble librarian stock, and because I asked a couple of questions about obscure reference books that I knew of from being a nerd, I got the job and was now officially a library page. I even got a raise a few weeks into the job. It happened because the state government raised the minimum wage, but a raise is a raise. It was right up my alley. My job was to take all the returned books and put them back on the shelves. Usually that took about an hour. Then I had a list of things I was supposed to do, like taking out the trash and cleaning the restrooms. Mostly I would sit and read.

So after school I would work at the library and on the weekends I would work at Six Flags. At the time I wanted to save up for a guitar, and that reason sounded good. But now I know better. I was really trying to avoid the reality that waited on me at home.

I played my guitar every day. I would go to school, then work after school. Then I'd come home. The plan was always the same. I would practice guitar for a little while and then start on my homework. But this never worked out in reality. I would always end up playing my guitar and losing track of time, and next thing I knew it would be bedtime. Homework was usually done during little gaps in the school day, and rarely done well. I didn't really care, though, to be honest. I had already dropped from being mostly an A student to getting mostly Bs. And I found that the level of work you had to do to barely get a B was significantly less than to try to get an A. It was a matter of efficiency. Why work my tail off to just miss getting an A when I could pretty much cruise to a B?

Meanwhile, Dad's hospital stay began to feel different. This visit I'm not sure the doctors ever really did anything. They ran a bunch of tests to see what they could do and decided they were out of options. I would go after school and just sit up there with him. Sometimes he would say something we didn't understand, but usually it was nothing. Other times he would reach above him with his hands, intently turning knobs that weren't there. It was as if he was doing something somewhere else, maybe some routine he had been used to doing at work. Mostly, though, trying to communicate with Dad was pointless.

That didn't stop Granddaddy from trying. "Jim, you know any good jokes?" or "When we going fishing?" he would ask, even though he knew he wouldn't get a response.

One day after school I had to run by the public library, which was only about a mile from the hospital, to get a book for school. I would have hated to admit it, but I had come to dread visiting Dad. I think I knew he was dying and I wanted to avoid it.

But still I sat up there with Dad one more time, getting nowhere as usual. After what seemed like forever, I got up and headed for the door.

"Dad, I gotta go. I have to get a book for school."

"Have a good time."

The fact that he responded at all shocked me, not to mention that what he said was kind of coherent and contextual.

That was the last thing Dad ever said to me.

● ● ●

Dad's condition had gotten progressively worse. After he had spent a couple of weeks in the hospital, the doctors were convinced they couldn't do anything more for him. Mom left the hospital one day with brochures about a couple of hospices. Then, on a sunny Friday afternoon in early May, we were checking Dad in at a Catholic hospice center in Atlanta. We were nearing the end.

I went down with Mom right after Dad got there. We took a tour of the grounds. While this was difficult to process, I figured I'd have some time to come to grips with it. Surely he would be there for a few weeks, even months. I knew that at some point I would have to deal with the inevitable. But it felt like there was time.

There wasn't.

That Sunday was Mother's Day. As I was getting ready to go to my shift at the amusement park, I got a call from Mom. She sounded upset.

"Your dad's not doing too good. They said he's taken a turn for the worse. I think you need to come down here."

I thought back to that call from the hospital just a little over a year ago. It seemed like only a few days ago, but so much had happened. Back then, there was a chance that Dad wasn't going to make it, and I worried. Now it seemed there wasn't a chance that Dad would live another day, and I was surprised to find a calm resolve within myself.

I drove down to the hospice and walked into Dad's room. Everything felt different. Dad looked lifeless and kind of gray. His breaths, which had come only with great effort for several weeks, were now accompanied by a disturbing gargling sound. I was told that this is called the "death rattle," and that it was a normal part of the process.

Normal. During this whole time all I'd wanted was normal, and now I was being told that death was normal.

Death is not normal. Maybe at one point it was more normal than it is, but people nowadays are just not exposed to it. However, it was normal at the hospice, which was something I was subjected to pretty quickly after I got to Dad's room. It was a semiprivate room with two patients separated by a curtain. When the nurse came to check on the other guy, she somehow was able to tell he was nearing the end. She called a couple of the other nuns in there, and they recited Psalm 23 and a Hail Mary. Then the nurse said, "OK, one more breath." How did they know he was about to die? How did they know when his last breath was going to happen?

I felt really bad for this man. At least we had our family there with us. Later that afternoon several of Dad's brothers and sisters drove up from Savannah, as did my mom's family from Elberton.

By that evening, we had twenty or thirty family members there, and it got crowded to the point that feeling crowded trumped my freak-out factor. Or maybe I had just forgotten. Before too long my cousin Beth and I were watching Aerosmith's *Rockumentary* on the TV on the other side of the room. Yes, this was in the same area where the other dude had died that morning. Before *Behind the Music* was MTV's *Rockumentary*, and it was epic. I was telling Beth all about the Aerosmith show I had just been to a week prior and how awesome it was. I was so wrapped up in this music documentary that I almost forgot we were in the room where a dude had just died a few hours prior, and just across the room from where my dad was dying.

The previous Sunday night I had seen Aerosmith at the Omni. This was the last gasp of normal for me. Or maybe not-normal was the normal. I drove my Camaro to the show. And on the way home, like clockwork, it broke down on the side of I-20. For someone who's been hit by a truck before, standing on the side of the interstate is as close to a worst-case scenario as I can imagine. Best I could tell from my now-expert car diagnosis skills, it was something with the transmission. I added some transmission fluid that I happened to have in the back of the car and was on my way. When you've got a car that breaks down all the time, you've got to travel prepared.

I had just finished sharing all this with Beth when Aunt Betty came over. "Mark, are you working at Six Flags again this year?"

"I am. I was actually supposed to work today, but Mom called me."

Right then I looked up and saw a couple of the nuns in there with Dad. They were crowding around him like they did with the other man earlier. As if something was about to happen. And of course, I knew what that *something* was.

"It's so great that Jim has so many friends and family members here. It's almost time," one of the nuns said. How did they know?

We all crowded around Dad's bed. His deathbed. Somebody, one of my aunts I think, stood behind me and reached out her hand. I grabbed it and think I might've squeezed the life out of it.

Dad's mom, my grandma Allie Fae, who I hadn't seen yet and didn't even know was there, sat down on the edge of the bed.

"It's OK, Mama's here now," she said, and kissed him on the forehead.

I remembered that it was Mother's Day, and this was how my grandmother was spending it. I don't know how sentimental she was. Was this how she would always remember it?

The nuns went into the same routine that they had with the other dude that morning.

"OK, one more breath," one said. How did she know?

And that was it. Dad was gone.

The nuns led us all in a recitation of Psalm 23, followed by a Hail Mary. This was a little different than what my church would have done, but it felt right. In those kinds of situations, nobody knows what to say. But it feels like somebody should say something. We clung to the Bible when there was nothing else to hold on to. And the nuns' faith would fill in during a time when we didn't have so much. It worked.

Somebody, maybe the same aunt whose hand I had squeezed the life out of five minutes ago, said, "Go kiss your daddy."

So I kissed my dad on the forehead. It was cold.

●●●

My memories of Dad aren't as defined as I wish they were. I remember a lot, but there's so much I've already forgotten. Not only have all of my memories of him grown fuzzy with age but all of those memories have this little clock at the top of them, reminding me of how long it would be until I'd lose him. I think of something happy from my childhood, and then I think something like *Wow, that was only five years before he died.*

Oh, look—there's me and my dad hiking at Kennesaw Mountain. The clock reminds me that he'll be gone in ten years. My dad's fortieth birthday party at our friends' house is filled with images of black balloons and candles and funny signs like "Lordy, Lordy, Jim is forty," and "Life begins at forty." But at the top of the screen of my memory, there's that little clock again, reminding me that his life, at least this chapter of it, would end in less than eight years.

I think about my dad every day. But the passing of time seems to fade the colors of the scenes my mind tries to paint of my childhood. I remember some events like landmarks. Then there are the hazier memories. Lastly are all those gaps in my memory where I don't really even know what happened anymore. And it's so frustrating that I can remember the phone numbers from stupid commercials from my childhood but I'm not even sure what color my dad's eyes were.

9

CROSSFADE

So rest awhile / It'll be alright
No one loves you like I do
I can't stop the rain / from falling down on you
  again
I can't stop the rain / but I will hold you till it
  goes away.

Third Day, "When the Rain Comes"

The lowest point of my life was not the day I got hit by the truck. It was not the day my father died. It was three days later. The day after his funeral.

Mom had let me stay out of school, which was probably a good idea. I needed an extra day to sleep in, to take it easy. School could wait another day.

The last couple of days had been crazy. We had a house full of company, and there always seemed to be something to do. Because I was old enough to drive, I was sent to do all kinds of things. Go to the gas station to pick up some ice, then to the grocery store to pick up some more chicken. I didn't have time to think about the Dad dying part.

On Monday, Mom, Jimmy, and I had to go to the funeral home to pick out a casket. It was so ridiculous—we all thought so. They had the different caskets arranged around the room like we were at a furniture store or a car lot. One of them was made of solid bronze. Another was stainless steel. Still another had a lifetime guarantee. Lifetime guarantee? I know Dad would have seen the humor in that one.

Then there was a visitation at the funeral home Monday night. They had Dad all laid out there in his casket, dressed up in a suit. Seeing him wasn't really very hard for me. He hadn't looked like himself in over a year, so this version, with a head bald from the radiation and chemo treatments and a face swollen from the embalming fluid, was not my dad. He had left us long ago, when the fog of brain cancer began to descend upon us.

We did the funeral on Tuesday. It was a beautiful, warm, sunny spring day in Marietta. Several of my teachers came to the funeral, as did many of my friends. I didn't really see anybody while we were in there, but afterward, as we sat in the car on that beautiful May afternoon, they came by and said hey.

When we headed out to the cemetery, a huge line of cars stretched out behind us. Knowing Dad, if he was going to have to die, he would have wanted it to be as big of a pain for other people as possible.

Back at the house, it was crowded and there were a lot of folks coming through. For the last year or so this had happened on a lower level, but now it was full-tilt. A bunch of chicken was eaten and I was sent out to get more. Then people started making their way back to Elberton and Savannah.

The worst day, three days after my dad died, was another painfully beautiful day, and I was sitting out on the back patio with a copy of *Huckleberry Finn* I was supposed to be reading for school. Try as I might, I just could not get into reading that day. I felt completely numb.

In front of me were two pine trees. A few years earlier, Dad had helped me nail a piece of an old garden hose between the trees as a makeshift goalpost. He was gone, but his work was still there.

Maybe that's what I was. Sort of a legacy of what he did while he was on the earth. I took a little bit of solace in that. Not much.

A few years before we had been in the backyard working on the lawnmower. Dad was fuming—something about having to work all day and then come home and work some more.

"Son, whatever you end up doing for your job, make sure you like it, because you have to do it every day," he said. This lone piece of work advice would become the backdrop for everything from here on out.

Grieving is a funny thing. My youth pastor during this time was right—when someone close to you dies, it's not a linear process of getting better. You never truly get over the pain, you just get used to it. I cried that night at the hospice, somewhere between Dad dying and the final prayers. That numb feeling I had the day after the funeral was really intense for a few days, and then lingered at a steady, lower level for months. In a certain sense, my senior year of high school, while I deliberately let it be fun, was all a big blur.

You know that feeling when you get in trouble and you have to sit out of a game, and then the teacher lets you rejoin your friends, and they're extra nice to you, and the game seems really fun, but there's kind of a falseness to it because you don't know if it's genuinely fun or if everyone's just being nice? That's how my senior year of high school felt.

Sometimes it was surprisingly easy how I could talk about losing my dad. Other times I would start talking about it and just couldn't because I would cry, and in high school that is decidedly not cool. This went on for a couple of years.

In music, there's a thing called a crossfade. One song will fade out and the next one will begin to fade in. It's an amazing effect when done well. It's just really hard. In Third Day we've done the trick where the song fades out and then fades back in, but I don't know about a crossfade. For me, grieving was like that. Some days I cried, some days I talked about it, and some days I felt some level of OK. But mostly I felt numb. I don't know when grieving ended and regular life picked back up. They sort of existed side by side for a while, and then there was just regular life left.

● ● ●

While it was hard to explain what I was going through to my friends while Dad was sick, things were surprisingly a little easier after he died. I didn't realize it until after it was over, but we had been in a holding pattern for the entire year before. As hurt as I was about losing Dad, as much as I knew I would miss him, on a certain level it felt like a release to not be in that holding pattern anymore.

I think what got me through this time were those landmarks in my life. Things that seemed firm, that gave me perspective. The world felt like it was shifting beneath my feet, and finding something solid to hold on to was the way I kept going.

Surprisingly, school ended up being a big part of that. While I had gotten burned out and jaded after feeling like I

Right after I got my first PRS guitar

sort of missed the program my first few years of high school, I really gave it a go after Dad died.

I remember my first day back at school, spring of my junior year. My teachers knew all about my dad's death, and I'm sure most of the other kids did too. I got the feeling that it had been talked about during my absence. While nobody really said anything to me specifically, everybody was really nice to me. And that made getting back into school a lot easier.

Mostly, I handled my father's death the way I handled everything else in high school: I pretty much avoided it. I simply kept my head down and tried to keep moving forward. One job wasn't enough—I had to keep two jobs going. So the rest of that spring and that summer, I was working. If I wasn't at the amusement park, I was at the library. If I wasn't at the library, I was at the amusement park.

Working at the library was a great excuse to get back to reading, which had been a key landmark when I was younger. In addition to re-shelving books, I also had an unofficial, unwritten goal to read, well, all of them.

"Mark, are you working or reading?" I was asked on more than one occasion. But the librarians were pretty cool about it. I don't think they really cared as long as I got all my work done.

All of these books with these crazy, cool titles would come through for shelving. As I sorted the books into their various

116

sections, I would make mental notes on what to read myself. For me, working at the library served as sort of a bridge from all the books I loved to read as a kid and the books I've read as a grown-up.

The 200s were the religious books. This is where I spent a lot of my time. Reading great books by new authors like Max Lucado as well as classics like John Wesley and C. S. Lewis helped me through this difficult season of life.

The 150s were the psychology books. These books were especially interesting to me because they unpacked a lot of what makes people act the way they do. They were also really encouraging to me during a time when I needed it.

I also discovered that I loved science fiction. I read great authors like Isaac Asimov, Carl Sagan, and Piers Anthony, along with the zany and the unclassifiable like Kurt Vonnegut and Philip K. Dick.

I remember reading Stephen Hawking's *A Brief History of Time* around this point and really loving it. I had really been into astronomy as a kid and this book was a cool way to keep my toe dipped in that water just a bit.

Finally, I loved the 780s. That small section of the library provided a vital crossroads between two of my favorite things in life. If I loved music and I loved books, the end-all, be-all, then, would have to be books about music. I devoured biographies of my favorite bands and found several interesting books of guitar music.

● ● ●

The fall of my senior year, I marched in the band again. It was generally known that several of us were in the marching band because it was the only musical outlet we had, and that quite a few guys in the marching band were aspiring rock musicians. We would talk about it all the time. We always talked about what we'd sound like if we were in a band. You could show off your musical knowledge and hipness all together. So we were always starting fake bands.

Somewhere along the way, I decided that Nuclear Hoedown was the coolest name for a band. Don't even think about stealing it—the name is copyrighted. I would write Nuclear Hoedown on my notebooks as if it were the name of a real band. I would write it on the dry-erase board in math class next to all the equations we were supposed to be learning. It felt right.

One afternoon before the first football game of the season, we had to stay after school and do a fitting for band uniforms. We had to wait our turn for the lady to take our measurements, and I was soon in the middle of an intense "what my band would sound like" conversation.

Mac Powell, who was the drum major, chimed in. "If I were going to start a band, I'd want it to sound like The Black Crowes."

I was impressed on several levels. First, the obvious: The Black Crowes were awesome. There had been a group of bands from Atlanta who had enjoyed some success. R.E.M., obviously, but also bands like The Georgia Satellites and Drivin N Cryin. The Black Crowes felt like a step forward in that tradition. I was also impressed that Mac wasn't afraid to say who he liked.

But mostly I was impressed that Mac even wanted to be in a band. I had only talked to Mac a couple of times and he hadn't struck me as a rock band kind of guy. I was intrigued.

Another of the trombone players, a guy named Jonathan, played bass and invited me to come over to his house and

Mac and I performing "Love Song" on the Revelation tour

jam with him and a couple of other guys. While I had been playing guitar for a couple of years by this point, I had no idea how I stacked up. I had always shied away from playing guitar in front of other people. Very few people even knew I played.

So I went over to Jonathan's house. His family had a spare bedroom that was partly Jonathan's practice room but mainly a weight room. I was greeted by Jonathan and two other guitar players. It seemed that everybody played guitar. I was handed the sheet music to a Megadeth song, straight out of a guitar magazine. Somebody counted us off and we all started playing. It sounded awful for sure. But alongside the awful there were flashes of something else, this cool other thing that I couldn't put my finger on, which happened when people made loud rock music together. While I don't think I played with Jonathan's band again—they already had two other guitar players—I was hooked.

All through my senior year, this informal music jam thing happened pretty often. There were a few guys I started getting together with after school on a regular basis. Kevin, a smart kid who somehow already had a full-time computer programming job while he was in high school, played guitar and was actually really good. Also, because he had a job he owned some cool gear, which is always a plus. I spent a lot of time hanging with Kevin. He had a little recording rig and we would make tapes of ourselves playing guitar. One day we worked up Jeff Healey's version of "While My Guitar Gently Weeps." While it definitely sounded like two high school kids playing, there was a spark of potential. And, like the golfer who plays a terrible round but has that one shot that makes him want to keep playing, it was a spark that kept us going.

Tim was one of my best friends from the marching band, and he had just begun to play the bass. I had a crush on his sister, so I spent quite a bit of time over there jamming with Tim. I don't think his sister was very impressed that I played guitar.

There was also this one kid who always brought an acoustic guitar to school. I'm not sure he ever played it. I think he hoped it would give him some air of credibility with the girls or something. I don't think it did. One day, while we were waiting for first period to start, I asked him if I could play his guitar. He shrugged and said sure, so I pulled the guitar out of the case and launched into the intro to "Crazy Train." This would later become very famous in Atlanta because they'd play it at Turner Field whenever Chipper Jones came to bat. At this point it was just a cool rock song. I was surprised that I wasn't really nervous playing in front of people, and while my classmates didn't exactly put me on their shoulders and parade me around the room, they didn't throw things at me either. It reminded me of playing fiddle at Uncle Larry's all those years ago—that thrill of playing in front of an audience.

● ● ●

As the crossfade continued from grieving back to regular life, the numbness I felt on that first day persisted. But alongside that, something else was at work. Those same landmarks that had helped me during this low point began to point toward where I might be headed in the future.

Getting hit by the truck and losing my dad had given me a distrust of happily ever after. Maybe it was because I was still young and didn't have the whole grown-up "I've got it figured out" thing going for me yet. Whatever it was, I didn't so much as give up on the idea as I had it knocked out of me.

But as I tried to pick up the pieces and move on with my life, this happily ever after idea would rear its head again and again. And each time I would discover that lurking underneath this beautiful lie was another ugly myth, another warped view of God and life that was getting in the way.

10

HIGH-WIRE ACT

I am walking on a wire / The pressure's getting
  higher
But I don't look around / It's so far to the
  ground.

Third Day, "Wire"

I have always been fascinated by high-wire acts. When I
was growing up, my parents loved driving in the North
Georgia Mountains. A frequent stop on our mountain ex-
cursions would be Tallulah Gorge, a massive chasm in the
earth carved out by the force of a river. If you go to Tallulah
Gorge you can still see the support towers from Karl Wal-
lenda's famous 1970 tightrope walk across the gorge. I saw
those when I was a kid, and my mind's image of what that
spectacle must have been like has stayed with me. The throngs
of people standing by the gorge's edge to catch a glimpse

of the man attempting this feat. The media frenzy it must have brought to this small north Georgia community. And the underlying question in the back of everyone's minds: *What if he falls?*

Years later I would write a song about this called "Wire," but that was just the culmination of it. Throughout my childhood it was something I thought about often.

In high school we had a retreat at church. One of the speakers told a story that stuck with me, probably because it was about a high-wire act. Back in the 1800s there was a famous tightrope walker named the Great Blondin. He walked across Niagara Falls on a high wire. Then he repeated the high-wire feat while wearing stilts. He did it again and made an omelet along the way. Finally, he got out a wheelbarrow. People in the audience shouted out "You are the best tightrope walker in the world!" He then asked who wanted to get in the wheelbarrow. Not a single person wanted to ride in the wheelbarrow with the greatest tightrope walker in the world.

Stories like this are a powerful tool. The Bible is full of stories, and the most famous are the parables told by Jesus. The thing about parables is that they often present a dilemma and there are several characters. You can take away a different life lesson every time you read a parable just by viewing it from the perspective of each different character. For example, it is a completely different story if you try to relate to the other brother as opposed to the prodigal son. Or if you view the Good Samaritan story from the perspective of the innkeeper.

At the retreat this tightrope walker story was presented as a modern parable, a lesson on faith: we are the people in the audience and we need to trust Jesus with the wheelbarrow.

But we can also read the story from the perspective of the tightrope walker. This also becomes a lesson in faith. But it's a different kind of faith. The tightrope walker trusts God to guide his every step as he's training. He starts as a boy, walking on boards in his backyard. Then he puts a rope up between two trees, maybe with a net underneath. After enough practice, he takes the net away. After years of training in this fashion, he starts performing in public, doing bigger and bigger stunts. By the time he takes his first step out onto that tightrope over Niagara Falls, it's the next logical step.

In my experience, that's how God's will works. He doesn't lay out the whole plan, he just shows us the next logical step. And he doesn't expect us to get off the couch and walk across Niagara Falls. He just wants us to take the first step and keep going. Keep putting one foot in front of the other. When we fall, he helps us get up. He'll reveal the rest of the way, one step at a time.

I do my share by doing everything I know to do and I trust God with the rest. The second part is the hardest. *God, why can't you just show me the whole path? Just lay it all out there so it's clear? And preferably easy?*

As I finished high school and began to think about what I'd do next, I had all these big decisions in front of me and I wanted direct answers from God about what to do, what the whole plan of my life would be. It didn't exactly work that way.

● ● ●

Our school was scheduled to have a talent show in the spring of my senior year. Some of my guitar-playing friends thought it would be a good idea to get something together for it. This was going to involve us transforming from a few dudes with guitars into an actual band. And you can't put together a band without finding the most vital element of all: a lead singer.

Just a few months prior, Mac Powell had turned a few heads, including my own, when he sang a Phil Collins song at a school assembly. At this point in time, his voice wasn't totally developed. Nowadays he has that deep baritone with that raspy quality people try to imitate. But it was much higher in tone back then, and he sounded just like Phil Collins. It was incredible. When you heard him sing, you weren't listening with that "he's just a kid" ear. He was genuinely good. With most people our age, you listened for potential. With guys like Mac it was already there.

Because I was in the marching band with Mac, it was decided that I would be the guy designated to make the talent show pitch. It was a good thing social skills weren't being judged at the talent show, because I had none. I was a skinny, shy kid who barely said a word in class. I was outgoing when I was with the marching band and in my element, but take me out of that and social interaction was a real struggle.

Between classes I went by the band building and saw Mac at his locker. I figured this was as good a time as any. At this point, I realized I didn't have any kind of speech prepared. I would just have to wing it.

"Hey, man. Do you want to be in my band? We're working up a song for the talent show."

Mac looked at me kind of funny. I genuinely thought he was going to say no. He probably already had some big plans for the talent show. He was probably going to wow everybody with a vocal performance. I was getting ready to tell him that it was OK; I understood.

"I can't play guitar," he said.

Of course. Mac knew that I played guitar. He was friends with some of the other guys I jammed with after school. So, of course, he figured that we'd be putting together a guitar thing.

"No, man. We want you to sing."

Mac's face lit up. "Sure. That would be great."

I don't really remember how after-school plans were made in those days. We didn't have cell phones, obviously. I guess you would call the person's house and leave a message. Or you would talk after school on the way out to the parking lot.

We got together at Mac's house. I had been to Mac's house a couple of times before for band parties. He had the perfect setup. The Powells lived in a split level kind of house, and his parents lived upstairs. Half of the downstairs was a garage and the rest was Mac's room. Sometimes we'd complete the rock and roll cliché and practice in the garage, but usually we'd just set up in Mac's room.

It ended up being Mac, Kevin, and me. We kicked around several of the metal songs that Kevin and I had been working on. Mac suggested that we try a Damn Yankees song that was big on the radio. But as we were listening to the song, it quickly became apparent it was going to be too high for Mac and that some of the lyrics were a little too dicey for a school function. Kevin and I were ready to give up on the song.

I was surprised by Mac's response. "Can you guys do it in a lower key?"

"Probably. But we still can't do the song. The lyrics are too raunchy."

"What if we rewrote some of the lyrics?"

As impressed as I had been with Mac's singing abilities, it was this other thing, this other knack he had, that set him apart from any of the other musicians I'd been working with. Indeed, it would set this apart from any other musical experiences I'd had.

I had grown up reading music. Anytime I performed, it was just that. I'd play something that was preplanned. If it wasn't on sheet music in front of me, I had memorized it from the music or from listening to a recording. But for Mac, if what he wanted wasn't there, he'd write it himself.

That talent show never happened. But we were invited, probably based on Mac's prior experience at the school assembly, to perform at a senior assembly in front of the whole school. On one hand it was amazing that we had this opportunity, but on the other hand it was terrifying. How many nightmares happen in front of the whole school?

When it came time to start working up a song, Mac surprised us again. He wanted us to perform a song he'd been working on called "Maybe the Next Rainy Day." He didn't know how to play guitar, so he sang the melody. Kevin tried to figure out the chords on guitar, while I sat down at the piano.

At one point we couldn't figure out a certain chord. Try as we might, there just wasn't a chord that fit the note Mac wanted to sing. We just found three notes that fit together on the piano. In hindsight it was a B7 chord. Paul McCartney once said in an interview that The Beatles rode across town on a train to find a guy to show them a B7 chord. Our rite of passage was a little easier. We just sort of pulled the chord out of the air on an as-needed basis.

This style of making music became the norm for us over the next couple of years. Most bands start out as cover bands, doing songs by other artists, and the jump to writing your own songs is as difficult as it is necessary. Today, when I sit down to play guitar, I don't have the repertoire of cover songs under my belt that many musicians have. That's because instead of focusing only on learning other people's songs, we wrote many of our own.

While I had been playing guitar for about three years by this point, I ended up playing piano instead for the school assembly. When we were working on the song, I had jumped onto the piano to help figure out a couple of chords. It sounded pretty cool, so we left it that way.

We did a soundcheck. I didn't know what I was supposed to do at a soundcheck, so I just kind of sat there. What I should have done was complain that we didn't have any monitors. When we actually performed the song, my keyboard sounded like it was about fifty miles away as it came out of those PA speakers in the New Gym. But we did the song, and we got through it.

I thought it was horrible. But afterward we got nothing but praise from people. They were blown away by Mac's voice and blown away that we had written the song. Like the band room conversation about The Black Crowes the previous fall, these comments were sort of filed away for future reference.

At the time, this felt like sort of a throwaway performance for us. The big thing we were looking forward to was Brian Waldrop's party. He had pulled me aside a couple of weeks prior to the end of school.

"I'm having an end-of-the-year party. It's going to be epic. We're looking for a band."

"Dude. I've got a band. Can we play?"

"Sure. Just don't blow it."

The common practice in those days was that if you were the one who secured the gig, you could pull the lineup together. So I invited Mac and Kevin. I also asked another friend, Chris. Chris could play all the intricate drum solos on Rush records. Another friend, Ray, played guitar but owned a bass, so he was recruited. As we began practicing for Brian's party, we decided to go without a dedicated bass player. Between us, we would switch out who would play bass. We met at Kevin's house one Saturday with a list of about thirty songs we wanted to play. Iron Maiden songs. Rush songs. We had been working on "Limelight" for several months, and it was kind of a go-to by this point. Mac shot it down. "That's a real crowd pleaser," he said, rolling his eyes. It was replaced by another song that was probably worse. But the idea of trying to put a show together rather than just playing songs that we wanted became important.

We were billed as Nuclear Hoedown. That name has become legendary, as if it was some great classic band that Mac and I cut our teeth playing in. The truth is, we were terrible. We didn't own a guitar tuner. We would tune once before the show and just go with it. While it was a good idea to work up thirty songs for Brian's party, any time we had a gig after that, which amounted to about three times, we would show up with a list of thirty new songs we wanted to learn. So we just never really got any good.

We did have a few bright spots. Anytime we would do a Southern rock song from a band like The Black Crowes or Drivin N Cryin or The Georgia Satellites, it felt right. It felt like us. We played that "Unbelievable" song and people seemed to get into that. And then we worked up a version of "Stayin' Alive" based on the Dweezil Zappa version of it that seemed to connect with other kids at these parties. That was about it.

● ● ●

As school ended forever and summer began, the musical opportunities kept coming. Nothing major. Just a party here and a party there. But we kept plugging away at it. I wouldn't go so far as to say we got good, but we got better.

Something else was happening over that summer. God was dealing with us.

Mac and I had several conversations about the Bible and about all the big things we were going through. I was still dealing with the loss of my dad. Mac was still trying to decide whether to go to college or join the military.

I'm always dwelling on big decisions, in the back of my mind, but when the time rolls around to actually make the call, I just go with it, like when my mom asked me if I wanted to play violin and I said yes without even thinking about it. So when I got my test scores back at the beginning of my junior year and realized I could go to Georgia Tech, that was it. I never took another test or applied to another school. It was a done deal.

But I could tell Mac was really grappling with these issues. And it was inspiring to me as well. His desire to read his Bible made me want to get mine out too. And I would read it and we'd talk about what we'd been reading. But this was all a natural thing. Writing songs, hanging out, and talking about heavy spiritual stuff all just seemed to roll in together. I never tried to separate them.

Somewhere around this time we were talking and Mac asked if I was a Christian. I told him about my experience while playing video games with my cousin. I told him about going through confirmation. I ended with telling him I was "as Christian as I was going to get."

"That's pretty sad," he said.

While that might sound a tad harsh, it meant a lot to me at the time. I knew he wasn't knocking my faith, and he wasn't saying that I wasn't a Christian. He was referring to my lack of commitment and the fact that I wasn't living it out that much other than showing up to church on Sunday.

Then Mac came to us one day and said he was quitting the band. I was devastated. Though our band sounds like no big deal now, just a little thing we did for fun in high school, at the time it was the most important thing in my life. We had big plans. We were going to go on tour in North Carolina. I don't know why. We didn't know anybody in North Carolina. But it seemed far enough away that it would count as "going on the road."

Many of the songs we were playing at this point were covers of songs that were popular on the radio. The lyrics of these songs were downright atrocious, and Mac wasn't comfortable singing them. He felt so strongly about it that if not singing them meant not being in the band, then that would have to be the route he took. He told me one day at his house while we were working on music.

My first reaction was anger, sort of. I totally got it. God was genuinely moving in Mac's life, and Mac felt like he needed to give up worldly things and get rid of his secular music. I joked and said I'd keep his CDs for him. The look he gave me said it was serious. I told him I understood, but I was still frustrated.

We got busy and I didn't see Mac for a while. I had foolishly quit working my library job at the end of high school, so I had to scramble around to find another job. I joined the marching band at Georgia Tech and started rehearsing for the coming football season. Mac did a couple of solo performances, including one at the local fairgrounds that was well received.

A couple weeks later Mac and I went to a concert with some friends. The Masquerade was a happening rock club during those days that often featured big-name bands we'd actually heard of. On off nights they would have all-ages shows, usually featuring local bands. For us, it was about the only place we were old enough to see live bands play. On this particular night it was just chaos onstage. The band that was playing, I forget the name, had TV sets all over the place, and there was a guy in the band whose sole job seemed to be running a grill and passing burgers out to people in the crowd. I thought it was hilarious.

For Mac, though, this show meant something different. I hadn't really been paying attention to the lyrics, but Mac had. This led to an interesting conversation on the way home from the show. Mac mentioned how awful some of the lyrics were. I should also mention that the lead singer had been dressed in drag. The other guys we were with took it all in stride and kind of ignored Mac.

After they left, though, Mac and I kept the conversation going. There was this lingering regret he had about quitting Nuclear Hoedown, and while he didn't want to go back, he couldn't think of another way forward.

Suddenly I had the solution.

"Do you want to start a Christian band?"

I don't know where those words came from, and to this day I don't know why I said them. I didn't know much about Christian music. My mom had bought me a Petra tape a couple years prior, which was pretty cool, and I was vaguely

In the studio working on the *Come Together* album

aware of Michael W. Smith, Amy Grant, and Carman. I wasn't even sure this was what I wanted to do, but it just felt like a way we could keep making music together without compromising our faith.

A few days later we were driving home from visiting friends at band camp in Carrollton. We stopped in at Turtle's record store and promptly marched to the Christian music section. Mac had heard of a band called Whiteheart that was supposed to be pretty good. The little music store didn't have much of a selection—there couldn't have been more than a couple dozen cassettes in the Christian section. They didn't have any Whiteheart, but they did have Whitecross. So we went ahead and bought it. It rocked. The scales fell from our eyes.

We would soon find ourselves binging on whatever Christian music we could get our hands on, drinking it in and making up for not having a childhood surrounded by this stuff. We discovered great artists like Rich Mullins, Whiteheart, and Steven Curtis Chapman, along with some not-so-good stuff. People loved to knock the quality of Christian music in those days, but I think it was just a case of Sturgeon's Law coming into play—most music in any genre isn't any good. And without much in the way of radio, there really wasn't a way to find the good stuff except through word of mouth.

● ● ●

A few weeks later we had our first rousing performance as a Christian band—on a flatbed trailer at Mac's church. It was a big youth event of some kind. We worked up a couple of songs, one of them being "Desert Rose" by Whiteheart and the other being a very loud version of "I'll Fly Away." We weren't very well versed in Christian music at this point, and being teenagers we didn't really have the budget to go out and buy new instruments, so we found ourselves with our '80s metal guitars trying to pull off a hymn.

I was humbled and flattered to see that my youth group came out to the show, as did several other friends from church and school. A good friend of ours, Vince Garrett, did the sermon that night. As he spoke, it felt like everything that had been going on for the last few months came together. The conversations Mac and I had, the things I'd been read-ing in the Bible, and my new interest in Christian music all seemed to point to the fact that I didn't need a commitment to music, I needed a commitment to Christ. So when Vince prayed and invited anyone who had made a decision that night to raise their hand, I proudly raised mine.

That summer I took every opportunity I got to play in front of people. At church they would host this thing once a month where the members of the congregation could get up and sing. The program was pretty loose but it basically meant that every few weeks I had a chance to play in front of people.

One Sunday I had no idea what I was going to play. I opened up a hymnbook. In between traditional songs, our hymnal had a few newer praise choruses complete with guitar chords. One of those was called "Seek Ye First," and it had a cool chord progression that I hadn't seen before. I decided to try that one.

The words to that song were a straight Bible verse, pulled from Matthew 6: "Seek first the kingdom of God and his righteousness, and all these things will be added unto you." Well, almost straight. There are a couple of alleluias added in there to make it sing right. But because of that song and that experience, I now know that Bible verse by heart.

Seek ye first.

I firmly believe that the commitment I made while playing video games was real. But this was the moment when I stopped striving to make something on my own, to become famous, to write my own story. This was the moment when I stepped into God's story, when I decided to use all my talents, and give all that I had for him—and to put that first.

All of the struggles, the doubts, the fears I'd had over the last few years didn't leave, but I had a newfound sense of hope that everything was going to be OK. Max Lucado talks about being in a boat with his dad during a storm and realizing that as long as he looked at his dad's face everything would be OK. My faith was like that.

I had been worried about making the big decisions and somehow still held on to the idea of some version of happily ever after, with a stretch of smooth sailing and a clear path ahead. But like the tightrope walker story, God doesn't show us the whole path, and what he shows is rarely clear. Yet he will show us the next step.

That numb feeling I had felt over the last couple of years was replaced by something else. It was something I couldn't wait to share with others.

Joy.

11

WHIRLWIND

"Go out and stand before me on top of the mountain," the LORD said to him. Then the LORD passed by and sent a furious wind that split the hills and shattered the rocks—but the LORD was not in the wind. The wind stopped blowing, and then there was an earthquake— but the LORD was not in the earthquake. After the earthquake there was a fire—but the LORD was not in the fire. And after the fire there was the soft whisper of a voice.

1 Kings 19:11–12 GNT

After the flatbed trailer youth rally thing at Mac's church, we performed at my church a time or two. Over the next several months we would play a couple of songs here and there for church services and youth groups. That December we were at Mac's girlfriend's birthday party. Mac came up to me.

"OK, I've been thinking about it, and I think I've got a great idea for a band name. What do you think about either Third Day or Three Days? Something like that."

I thought it sounded pretty cool. We asked a few other folks at the party. Most of them thought we could come up with something better. But we never came up with anything better, and I'm so glad. I love that our band name and our faith are wrapped up together like that.

Mac and I started writing songs. We had a friend named Billy Wilkins who played keyboards with us. Billy was a few years older. He taught business at McEachern and was also the youth pastor at Mac's church. Billy brought an element of fun to the band. Whenever we set our gear up on a stage, Billy would find the most out-of-the-way, unseen place to set up his keyboards. Mac would bring a video camera and record our shows. So many times we would watch the video after the show and Billy would be set up behind a plant or something, and we would laugh until we cried.

Billy was a great keyboard player—he could play gospel piano like nobody's business. More importantly, he was a great mentor to us. So many of our practices in those early days would turn into a Bible study or a prayer meeting. A lot of people to this day want to know the secret to starting a band that's going to be successful. While obviously there are no guarantees, it certainly didn't hurt things that we spent so much time in prayer and studying Scripture. We genuinely tried to live out what we were talking about in our songs.

I suppose the plan was that we were going to recruit some other guys besides Billy to play in the band. But then we saw Rich Mullins do a show in Atlanta. To my memory, Rich didn't have drums on this show. He had acoustic guitars and

A mini-reunion with keyboardist Billy Wilkins

mandolins and a hammer dulcimer. We saw that and decided that's what we wanted to do. So I bought a mandolin, and for Christmas that year I got a mountain dulcimer. All of our performances up to that point had been acoustic by necessity—it was usually just Mac and me—but from then on we were acoustic by design. The idea of getting a drummer went on the back burner.

Third Day's first official show happened at a little place in Cherokee County, north of Atlanta. We saw some friends of ours perform a show there and thought this might be a great venue for us to do a full-length show. The place was in the basement of some kind of plumbing business or something. I am not sure of the whole story. But they would host Christian concerts there. It was a word-of-mouth kind of thing, but I do know a lot of people would come out to the shows. So, after one of the shows, we asked the guy in charge and he put us on the books to play there in March. The guy asked what time we wanted to get there and I said, "How about three o'clock?" He was fine with that.

What I didn't realize at the time was that when you are setting up and sound checking for an acoustic show you really only need about half an hour, especially if the sound system is already set up. If maybe it was really rough going, it still would only take an hour. And so we got there about three hours earlier than we needed to. Which gave me about three hours to experience something I never had before.

Stage fright.

I do not know what the deal was. I used to get nervous before violin recitals because it was just me up there, and everybody has nightmarish visions of getting up in front of people and all kinds of horrible things happening. But ever since about the sixth grade, when I started performing in the band at school, and even when I did solos, I didn't really get nervous. If I got nervous leading up to it, I would think, *What can I do about it?* My only answer was to practice more. So I would get a certain level of practice under my belt and then I would just trust that what was supposed to happen would happen.

But now, getting up there and singing our own songs suddenly felt entirely different. It felt like if the audience didn't like Third Day then they didn't like me. So I was just a ball of nerves, and I probably played pretty terribly. But, as I quickly learned, a lot of the bands who played these kinds of things really didn't have any business being up there. And the audience was looking at our potential more than anything else—and at our hearts. And in our hearts we were excited to tell people about Jesus. I think that was the biggest idea people took away from that first concert.

Somebody who came to the show in Cherokee County invited us to play at their church, and we agreed. After we played at that church, somebody asked us to play for their youth group. There always seemed to be another gig on the horizon. And that was sort of our existence. We never thought too terribly much about the future. We just focused on getting ready for the next show, and the one after that.

That first summer we did finally start looking for a drummer. We realized that even though we wanted things to be acoustic, we still wanted the power that comes from a full band. We put out an ad in a local music magazine and fielded several calls. We even had a couple guys come out and play with us for a show. The next week after that, when we were scheduled to practice, the new guys never showed up. To this day I joke that one day those guys are going to show up at rehearsal and say, "OK, we're ready to rock."

If you look on our website, you can see the flyer from an event called Holly Fest 1992. It happened at Hollydale Church, and at this point in time this was the biggest show we had ever done. In addition to bands, there were speakers. I think there might have even been a magician on the bill. They pulled out all the stops and got a big, local Christian band called Redline. Third Day got to be in the second slot. Also one of the ladies in the church was cousins with one of the singers in a group called the Bullard Band.

I sat out in the crowd and watched the Bullard Band. It was really strange to think that this was the same little church I grew up in, but I think I was mostly just excited about playing a show. As I was reminiscing about that, I noticed that the Bullard Band had a couple of what looked like high school kids in the band. Sure enough, as the band went around and introduced themselves between songs, both of those guys introduced themselves by saying they were in high school.

After the show, one of the guys in the Bullard Band introduced himself to us. His name was Mark. He played guitar and sang, and he talked about our potential and asked if we'd ever made a recording. We hadn't. I mean, we had certainly talked about it quite a bit, but had never followed through. Mark mentioned that David, the drummer for the Bullard Band, was in his youth group and possibly could help us make a demo recording. As payment, perhaps we could do a show for Mark's youth group?

I am so thankful that we cultivated the habit of prayer, even in those early days. Mark was certainly an answer to prayer. I am also thankful that he was faithful to the voice of the Holy Spirit in that moment. I'm sure he just as easily could have ignored it. But that conversation would mark the beginnings of Third Day as we know it.

Whenever anyone asks us about the beginnings of the band, that's the time we give them. Even though Mac and I had been doing shows as Third Day for a year or so, it didn't become a band until we had David as our drummer.

A few days later we found ourselves in the basement of David Carr's house, rehearsing for this show for Mark Manuel's youth group.

We performed the show and soon after started working on a demo with David. Unbeknownst to Mac and me, one of the kids in the crowd at the youth group show was named Tai Anderson. He was the bass player for the Bullard Band, and he and David were close friends. During the recording process, David suggested we recruit Tai to play bass. Tai showed up one Saturday a few weeks later to lay down his bass tracks. This day just so happened to be the day that we were being photographed for a promotional kit we were putting together. Tai was there that day, so Tai was in the pictures. There was never even really a discussion. Third Day was now a five-member band with a bass player.

This process of one show leading to the next would continue for about three more years. We only made a couple of cold calls during this time. I called a guy named Marty Bush, who ran a local music magazine. Marty was also starting a rock club called the Miracle Theater. I called him to see if we could perform there. Well, actually I first contacted him about playing a festival he did called Inner Seeds. We auditioned and were invited to play. There was just one problem. Apparently they had us double-booked with another band. I don't know why we didn't raise more of a fuss about this. We just said "OK" and went on our way. Maybe Marty felt bad about that—though I actually doubt he even knew about it—but when we made the call to see if we could play at his new rock club he obliged. A year or so later he started a record company called Gray Dot Records and invited us to be on it.

Another call we made was to a guy at David's church named David Mardis. David was a local engineer who had worked on a couple of big pop and hip-hop records. He came by and watched us rehearse—this time we moved our operation to Tai's basement—and liked what he saw. David Mardis acted as our producer and manager for a couple of years and was a big help in getting us to the next level.

● ● ●

One of the most interesting parts of a typical *Behind the Music* episode is when the band starts taking off. You see the band get together, then maybe they play a couple of small local shows. Then all of a sudden—*bam*—they're huge. It feels like a couple of steps get skipped.

I think it's because there's a phenomenon in the career of a musician where a bunch of big things happen over a short period of time. You put out a record and you promote the record, and you go from doing maybe a couple dozen shows a year to over a hundred. And time itself feels like it's moving at a different pace—everything happens so fast and you don't really have time to stop and figure out what's going on. It's like surviving an endless progression of whirlwinds.

One of my favorite passages in the Bible is the story of Elijah. Elijah demonstrated the power of God in a big showdown on top of Mount Carmel with the prophets of Baal. Even though Elijah "won" the contest, he went into a general funk. For years. Then God brought him up a mountain and had him hang out in a cave. A big violent whirlwind went by, but God wasn't in it. Then a gentle wind came by, and that was filled with the presence of God. While we love to focus on the big and the flashy, that's not the place to look for God. More often than not he reveals himself in the calm of the everyday.

The first whirlwind happens when the band is starting to take off. You are still trying to juggle life and the music, and as busy as you are with the music, you still have to keep a job to support yourself, or maybe you're still in school.

The whirlwind kicks up even stronger when you put out a record and start touring and your whole world gets turned upside down. A lot of musicians make bad decisions during this time and mess up their lives.

They don't talk about it in the music documentaries, but this is the most critical point in the life of the band. If you can survive these whirlwinds, if you can handle the success and the craziness and the busy, and listen for God in the gentle wind, you have a good shot at making it. Otherwise, who knows.

I'm talking about this from a band perspective, because that's what I know, but I'm pretty sure this phenomenon could happen to anybody. You set a goal and you go after it hard, and happily ever after becomes the accomplishment. After that, it'll all be downhill.

The problem is that it's not all downhill. You think once you get what you're going after that it's going to be easy. Instead, all the dynamics in just about every relationship in your life will change. Suddenly you are faced with an entirely new set of problems.

Once again, God comes through with landmarks. When the way gets rough and we start to lose ourselves, these landmarks guide us forward, reminding us of where we were really going. By the same token, when things get really busy and crazy and we're getting knocked around in all different directions and it would be easy to get blown off course, these landmarks keep us grounded and remind us who we are.

Obviously, faith is the biggest of these landmarks. The budding faith I had when I was younger really started to grow as the band gained more attention. I really wanted to live the kind of life we were singing about. I renewed my relationship to God. I took my faith seriously, reading the Bible and praying every day.

Prayer is a huge part of faith, and it's something we relied on quite a bit. Whenever Mac gives advice to young musicians, he always tells them to play together, taking any opportunity that comes their way. But more importantly, he also encourages them to pray together, seeking God's wisdom and direction both individually and collectively.

This idea really hit home for us when we felt like we were stuck. When we signed with Gray Dot Records, we were young and excited about going in the studio. We didn't really dwell too much on the details of our contract. We later realized that we'd agreed to a long-term contract with them. For recording one album while we built a following, Gray Dot was fine. But for the long haul, it was not going to be a good situation.

The record company sold through their stock quickly but it would be a long time before they ordered more. So we were out promoting an album that people couldn't buy.

We were out on the road, working hard, and getting really frustrated. We actually considered breaking up. But God put some great people in our lives who encouraged us to pray. We prayed with several people after shows. After a show in St. Louis, we prayed with some youth pastors in a church parking lot, and they encouraged us to be specific in our prayers. And so we prayed that God would help us sign to Reunion Records. So many of our favorite artists like Rich Mullins, Michael W. Smith, and Wes King were on that label. If we had to name our perfect dream scenario, this would be it. Why not be honest and ask God for what we really wanted?

A couple of months later, our contract with Gray Dot was bought out, and we were signed to Reunion Records.

Relationships are another landmark. When you're a kid, your primary relationships are with your family. Throughout school, you may go through different friends, but family is still a big deal. As you grow up, that sort of evolves to where the lines between friends and family get kind of blurred. You have family relationships that evolve into friendships and friends who feel more like family.

The more we toured and the more we went through together, the more the guys in Third Day became like brothers to me. I remember one time in particular when we were doing an interview. I think the interviewer had asked about the importance of a man's relationship to his father.

"I have a little different story than a lot of people, because I lost my dad to cancer," I began, and was surprised by the wave of emotion that I felt swelling up. "People take it for granted that they'll always have their dad in their life," I said. Then I just lost it. I couldn't get any more words out through the tears.

After the interview the other guys all hugged me. Along with missing my dad, I think a lot of it was that I was thinking about how much those guys meant to me and that I didn't want to lose them either.

Right when the whirlwind started to kick up real good, I decided I needed to quit the band.

12

SECRET OPTION C

We have grown up in an either/or universe, and we must
move into a both/and universe.

Madeleine L'Engle

I have long been a fan of Madeleine L'Engle. When I was
a child, her novel *A Wrinkle in Time* rekindled my imagination at a critical time when it threatened to die out for
good. And somewhere along the way I discovered that she
wrote several books for adults as well. Reading these books
continued to push the frontiers of faith and imagination for
me like nothing else.

In a world of cut-and-dry, black-and-white, L'Engle brings
a refreshing sense of open-mindedness. I have a lecture of hers
on audio that I listen to frequently. In this talk she addresses
the idea of either/or. In so many of our questions about life,
we come to God and give him exactly two options: either/or.

L'Engle reminds us of Jesus. Oftentimes the teachers of the law came to Jesus and tried to trip him up with an either/or question. Jesus wouldn't play their game. Instead he would answer with a mind-blowing secret option C.

"Jesus! Is it this? Or is it that?"

And Jesus, as only Jesus could, would say something like, "A fox has a den and a bird has a nest, but the Son of Man has no place to lay his head."

In more situations than I can count, happily ever after has reared its ugly head as an either/or. I have this big decision weighing on me and there are exactly two ways it can go. It's either this, or it's that. One of these paths leads to happily ever after. The other? Well, it can only lead to a place where there is much wailing and gnashing of teeth.

And how many times does it actually end up being one or the other? Not very many. More often than not, I've found that if I do what I know to do and just trust God with the rest, he'll come through with that mind-blowing secret option C. That's just how he rolls.

Now when I am faced with an either/or, before I decide, I try to look for a both/and. Do I *have* to decide? Is there a way to do both?

● ● ●

For a long season I was in school at Georgia Tech, then going to one of a myriad of part-time jobs I held, and then going to practice with the band. On the weekends we usually had a show.

Something had to give. The band felt like a once-in-a-lifetime kind of thing I couldn't let go of. The job thing was important, because, well, I had to have money to get by. Should I quit school, then? Mom would be devastated. So I took a bend but don't break approach and just let it ride as long as I could.

One day, during all of this, I came by Mac's house to drop off some of the cassettes we'd recorded with David Carr. Mac had some friends from his job over to watch a movie or something. I didn't really think much about it until I was starting to leave.

"You need a haircut."

Startled and taken aback, I turned around to see who had said that. It was one of Mac's friends, a girl named Stephanie.

"I'm going to get it cut right now," I shot back with a smile.

As luck would have it, I really was on the way to get it cut. For my entire freshman year of college I had been growing my hair out, and it had gotten quite long. Then I had to get it cut for some job or another and had gone to one of those five-dollar haircutting places. Let's just say I got my entire five dollars' worth. That evening I was literally on the way to have it cut properly.

Later that summer, Mac and I were going with a couple friends to visit his parents' lake cabin in Alabama. Right before we left, I found out that Mac had invited some of those girls who worked with him to go on the trip. I rolled my eyes, but then had this thought hit me: *I'm going to marry one of them.*

It ended up being a fun trip. And, sure enough, one of my favorite parts about the time was being able to hang out with Stephanie. She and I picked at each other literally from the start, and just hit it off as friends.

By the end of that summer, Stephanie and I were officially dating.

By about mid-1994 I was really feeling the pressure of my schedule. Between school, work, the band, and the increasing time I was spending with Stephanie, there weren't enough hours. We had begun work on another set of demos in David's basement. We had learned quite a bit the first time around, and were now having fun with some new songs. Our sound had progressed from the acoustic thing we had tried to do after seeing Rich Mullins. Most of the shows we played at that time were for youth groups, and the kids didn't really seem to get into the acoustic as much. Our songs were getting more and more rock, in the vein of bands like Pearl Jam and The Black Crowes. We even started adding some electric guitars to the mix.

It all came to a head for me as we were driving home from playing at Camp High Harbour one weekend. Mark Manuel, who had introduced Mac and me to David and Tai a year or two prior, was driving us home in a van. It had been a great trip, performing for the counselors there who were getting ready to work at the camp that summer.

Mark had invited us to perform for YMCA camps he worked with in the North Georgia Mountains a few times. By far our favorite was Camp High Harbour. It was a beautiful camp on the shores of Lake Burton. Every Friday night in the summer they held a big bonfire for the campers. We played for them a couple of times, and could really sense something special going on at this camp.

After this show at their leadership retreat we hung out with Ken, the head of the camp, and really hit it off. He had us play for another event at the camp a few weeks later, and presented us with an enticing offer: we could work at the camp that summer as their house band.

Tai had been talking to Ken, and they had devised a pretty cool plan. Third Day would be the house band at camp that summer. We would perform three times a week for several

151

Performing at Camp High Harbour

hundred campers from all over Georgia and the southeast. In addition to that, the camp had connections with other camps as well as some other local businesses where we could play.

And we would still be free to perform regular Third Day shows. By this time Marty Bush had moved his club to a cool theater in downtown Marietta called The Strand—we'd be free to play there on Saturdays. And if a big enough gig presented itself, we would be given the opportunity to break away from the camp for a few days.

The conversation went in a little circle around the van, as guys were tossing out different reasons why it would be the best thing for our career. I was quiet. I'm always quiet in meetings. A lot of that centers around the fact that I'm not very good at coming up with ideas in real time. While I do rely on that split-second intuitive decision-making thing for big decisions, it's harder to use in everyday situations. So I usually end up being sort of a muller, a percolator. I come up with good ideas, but they usually happen as the result of reflection. Definitely not on the spot.

After a while, the others began to notice that I wasn't saying anything.

"Mark, what do you think?"

Think, think. I didn't know what to think.

"No comment," I sort of blurted out, trying to buy myself some extra time.

But the others thought that "no comment" meant I was opposed to the idea. That wasn't the case at all. It really did sound like a great plan.

I stared out the window. The stars were brighter up here than at home in the suburbs. The moon was out, and you could see the silhouette of the mountains against the night sky. I've always loved the mountains, and it would be so cool to live in them for a summer.

But up to that point I had been set on going to school that summer, really hunkering down so that I could be done sooner. Stephanie and I had been dating for almost a year, and it was very serious. Did I really want to leave her for that long?

This decision about camp seemed to be a decision about what I wanted to do with my life. I felt like if I said yes to it that would mean saying no to everything else. I wouldn't come out and say that, but it seemed that if it was either the band or everything else, then I was going to have to choose everything else.

Mark always did a good job of helping us talk through things. I remember him saying something that I have often repeated: "We don't have to decide right now." He also encouraged everyone to not have a "Mark bashing session," even though I was the only one who didn't seem to be on board with the idea. He encouraged us to pray about it, right then and there in the van.

As we went around our little makeshift circle and prayed, I glanced out the window again. On the side of the road was a car, or what was left of it, completely engulfed in flames. The flames seemed to come up from the road in waves, shooting through the car and up toward the sky. My heart went out to whoever had been in the car, and I silently began to pray for their safety. I could also relate to them, because it felt like my life was going up in flames too.

We prayed that night, and a few days later we were in a friend's studio, working on some music, and we prayed about it then too. We all agreed that I would leave the band, and everybody seemed to be pretty supportive.

A few days later I called Mac, and he told me about a guy they had met named August, who was a great guy and a really good guitar player. Mac wanted me to stick around for a few more months to make sure everything was cool with August.

Making a pun on a Counting Crows album title, I told Mac, "Good luck with August and everything after."

My last show was supposed to be that May at a local college. August pulled me aside before the show. "Is it normal to be nervous?" he asked.

"Absolutely. The best thing I can tell you is that over time, whatever can go wrong, will go wrong. So don't worry about it. Just have fun." I guess all I could muster up was some kind of warped version of Murphy's Law. But I hoped everything would work out great with the band. And I genuinely hoped August would work out. He was a good guy.

Sometimes you don't realize it until you look back on things, but it is amazing to see how God is in control. And so many times, what looks like an either/or to us is a both/and in the eyes of God. I quit the band, planning on never looking back, but God had other plans.

I stayed around to help August get used to playing in the band, and around this time we started recording with David Mardis. While the recordings we had done a few months prior were fun, this felt like a major step forward. It felt like a real album. I played acoustic guitar on most of those songs and electric on a couple others.

This recording project epitomized the whirlwind season we were in. We would record all night at a studio in Atlanta. I would crash at the studio while other tracks were being recorded, then I'd leave straight from the studio and go right to class. At some point in the middle of the project I had a French history test. I hadn't studied for it at all so just relied on my memory from the lecture. Somehow, I managed to get an A on that test. Later I wouldn't be so fortunate.

That summer, the other guys gave me a standing invite to play at the camp whenever I could. Every Friday night the band would play as part of the big closing ceremonies for that week's camp. I went to all of those except maybe one. We played The Strand once or twice a month, and the crowds were bigger every time. I never missed one of those shows either.

By the end of the summer, two things were apparent: things weren't working out with August and I wasn't leaving the band. So God wasn't done using me in the context of Third Day after all.

I jumped back into the band with both feet and a new commitment. We kept doing shows and were starting to get more and more gigs. By this time, through all the shows at The Strand and David Mardis's work, we were also starting to get more and more attention. Our shows expanded from Georgia to neighboring states, even as far away as Oklahoma and Texas.

Here I was in this amazing position, where the band I had built up on the side was seeing enough success that it was getting in the way of school.

What was I going to do about school?

● ● ●

I read somewhere that Amy Grant went to Vanderbilt for a while but had to quit when she found she wasn't able to keep up with her studies. As I continued to juggle the band with attending college full-time, I figured that Amy must have hit some point where she just knew she couldn't keep up. I just assumed that when that point hit for me it would be pretty obvious.

The kicker for me was the next spring, when I was taking a Chinese history class. It was actually really interesting—a lot of Chinese kids took the class as an elective, so it was almost all Chinese students plus me and two or three other history majors. It was a pretty regular occurrence that the professor would switch back and forth between English and Mandarin mid-lecture. Really fun, really fascinating class. But I had to miss it. A lot.

One day I walked into class after missing several in a row. On the whiteboard behind the professor were the words "Final Exam! Wednesday June 7 at 2 PM!" The exclamation marks told me it was important, so I furiously copied this down in my notebook. *I may miss a bunch of classes, but I'm not going to miss the exam*, I thought.

I ended up missing quite a few more classes, but I pretty much kept up with my reading assignments and so I felt somewhat adequately prepared for the final exam. On Wednesday, June 7, at 2:00 p.m., I marched proudly into Room 201 of the Smith Building at Georgia Tech. What I found waiting for me was an empty classroom with all of the lights turned off. I waited for a while to make sure I wasn't just running early, but no one showed up.

Oh, so this is what it's like to be behind in my studies. Maybe this is where Amy Grant made her graceful exit. Maybe it's time to make mine.

A few weeks later we were getting ready to do our album release party at The Strand. Right before it, I had perhaps the hardest conversation I've ever had with my mom.

"Mom, with all the time I'm spending on the band, I'm really struggling in school. Something's got to give."

In her eyes I could see a glimmer of hope that maybe I'd quit Third Day and focus on school. But in her heart she knew what I was going to tell her.

"I'm going to put school down for a while. I can always come back."

I'll never forget her reaction.

"No. You can't be a musician. Musicians are weird."

She was pretty right about that.

But up to that point, this had been the goal, the happily ever after of my childhood that I had continued to hold on to, albeit with an ever-loosening grip: finish college, get a good job, live happily ever after.

From about fourth grade on, when I had told my teacher I wanted to be an inventor and she said, "You should go to Georgia Tech and become an engineer," that's what I had wanted to do. Even though I'd changed majors, my goal was to finish school at Georgia Tech.

While I knew giving up that goal was the next logical step, at the time it sure felt like that step was out onto a high wire over Tallulah Gorge.

Secret option C: graduating from Grand Canyon University

If you're following along at home, at this point you might be thinking *Aha! It was an either/or after all! He chose the band over school.*

It did feel like it at the time, but many years later, Third Day partnered with Grand Canyon University to put on a tour. As part of the deal, we got the opportunity to go back to school.

In June 2013, I received a degree in Christian studies from Grand Canyon University. At a show in Prescott Valley, Arizona, they held a special graduation ceremony. The dean of students came out and presented Tai and me with our diplomas. We wore caps and gowns. As we walked off the stage, confetti cannons went off. It was one of the most memorable nights of my life.

Secret option C.

13

FAIRY TALES ARE JUST THAT

The ordinary way to holiness and to the fullness of
Christian life is marriage.

Thomas Merton, "Vocation"

When most of us think about the phrase "happily ever
after," two things come to mind. First, the classic
fairy-tale ending: the knight saves the princess, they live happily ever after, blah, blah, blah.

Second, marriage: it gets talked about and dreamed about
from that same tender age when we still believe in fairy tales.
People see a beautiful wedding and describe it as a fairy-tale
wedding. So the expectations surrounding weddings, and the
marriages that follow, are nothing short of fantasy.

I wanted my marriage to Stephanie to be absolutely perfect. So much so that I wanted to wait until the perfect time
to propose to her. That never happened.

Stephanie and I. It hasn't been happily
ever after, and it hasn't been perfect, but
it's been pretty close!

In the summer of 1996 we were doing a show in Columbus, Georgia. It was close enough to Atlanta that most of us drove ourselves to the show. Stephanie and I made the drive from Atlanta. We listened to some music, but I remember the drive as being mostly silent. As we neared the venue, a big Baptist church that was expecting a sold-out crowd, I began to sense that something was on Stephanie's mind. As we were pulling into the church parking lot, Stephanie turned to me with tears in her eyes and said, "I am so proud of you for living out your dream, but what about my dream? What about our dreams together?"

Not long before that the band had a meeting with a new management team in Nashville. One of the guys asked us if anybody was married. Brad, our guitar player, had gotten married a few months prior, but no one else was.

"Good," the manager said. "I think the rest of you guys ought to stay in a holding pattern for a while."

That sounds crazy now, but at the time it made total sense. The whirlwind was in effect and the band was dominating our time. But the timing of getting married isn't necessarily one of those sensible decisions you make. I'm not saying that doubts never enter the picture, but you just kind of know. That's how Stephanie and I were.

But still, I wanted it to be perfect.

Near the end of 1996, Tai and I had the weirdest conversation. We knew that both of us would get married sometime in the next year. And at that point Third Day had exactly two free weekends in 1997. So Tai took one and I took the other.

I had a friend who worked at a jewelry store and could get me a deal on a diamond. Deals are a big deal when you're a fledgling musician. It sounded perfect. Until it took several months for the diamond to ship.

I wish my wedding proposal story was perfect and Pinterest-worthy, but it's not. Unfortunately it happened out of practicality. Stephanie's mom was leaving to go out of town for several weeks with her job and I wanted to talk to Stephanie's parents before she left. So on a Thursday night I went over to Stephanie's house while she was at work and asked their permission.

As I was explaining how I hoped to provide for their daughter with my meager musician's salary, her dad thought for a minute. Then, with a completely straight face, he said, "I guess you could go on *Jeopardy!* if y'all ever needed some money."

Knowing that perfect was out and plan B was in full effect, I ditched the idea of waiting on the diamond to come in. I hastily went to a little gift shop near my house and bought a fake ring for $25.

The next night I took Stephanie to a place called Ray's. The internet existed at this point in time, but I didn't own a computer. So I wasn't able to do the research to figure out that it was a seafood place. Stephanie hates seafood.

So then I took her to a place called the Polaris. If you've ever seen the Atlanta skyline and wondered what that weird blue spaceship–looking building is, that would be the Polaris. It used to have a commanding view of the skyline, but unfortunately all the buildings grew up around it, so by this time the views weren't quite what they used to be.

But at least the restaurant rotated. The problem with a rotating restaurant is that it's completely round. And the acoustics of this completely round restaurant made it possible to hear perfectly what the people on the exact opposite side of the restaurant were saying. Now I've always been shy, and I'm still shy to an extent, but I was really shy back then. So as I was working up the nerve to propose to Stephanie, I kept hearing these strangers talking from up in the ceiling.

I finally broke down and popped the question. But the voices in the ceiling had me rattled. The big, amazing speech I had in my mind was replaced with something like this:

"I was wondering if you wanted to be my wife."

I was wondering? What? While the songwriter in me got some points for all those alliterative Ws, I had struck out as a romantic. Fortunately for me, Stephanie looked past my blunders and said, "Yes."

From up in the ceiling, all the strangers at that other table let out a collective "Awwww."

● ● ●

There are a couple of telling photographs taken on our wedding day. In one, you see a line of people waiting to get into First Methodist Church. It's a cute picture, driving home the point of how many people were at the wedding. But above the brick church with its white steeple and weather vane is a dark and foreboding cloud. In another photo taken that day, Stephanie and I are beaming at the camera, standing in front of the limo that would drive us to the reception. In the background, you can see a hearse driving by.

Were these pictures some kind of portent pointing toward an unhappy, failing marriage? Absolutely not. We've been

Stephanie and I on our wedding day (See the hearse in the back!)
[Photo credit: Carney Photography]

married for twenty years now, and they have unequivocally been the best years of my life. Were the pictures a sign that maybe our wedding day wasn't going to go off without a hitch, that maybe I should let go of this idea of perfect? Absolutely.

Our actual wedding ceremony was short and sweet. If I say so myself, it really was a fairy-tale wedding. After taking some pictures with family, we were picked up in a hip 1940 Cadillac limo. The driver was your prototypical Southerner.

"Y'all don't want to get to the reception first, do you?" he drawled. "You'll have to wait on everybody. You want me to stop and get y'all a Coke?"

Stephanie and I looked at each other. "Sure!" we said at the same time. This marriage thing was easy.

163

He stopped at a gas station and got us drinks before heading toward the reception. Just after we bumped across the railroad tracks into the old Marietta Square, we drove across a through street. As we were crossing the intersection we heard a strange clanking sound. The limo stopped. We had gotten in a fender bender. Nothing major—the limo driver and the other car exchanged numbers. I think we even said at the time, "This will make a great story. Those people got in a wreck with a wedding party."

We went to the reception at the local country club and it was great. We had another little hiccup when we were cutting the cake and the knife broke, but no big deal. We danced with our parents. We danced with our friends. We ate food. Well, somebody ate food—I was too busy talking to really eat much. We took photos with friends and family and a bunch of people I didn't know.

We left the reception and headed to Stephanie's parents' house to change and grab our bags for the honeymoon. We got there and realized we didn't have keys. But again, this is another of those "It makes for a great story" kinds of moments. We eventually got inside, changed, and then headed down to a hotel in Atlanta. The nice limo driver dropped us off at the curb. Thinking I'd read somewhere that you're supposed to tip the limo driver and a lot of wedding couples forget this, I grabbed my wallet. I was supposed to have several hundred dollars. It was empty. This had to be a joke. I frantically called my brother to see if maybe it really was some kind of ha-ha groomsmen prank. I knew it wouldn't be, because that didn't sound like something my brother would do. In calling him I soon discovered that whoever took my cash had also stolen my brother's credit card and had already begun using it.

I realized, to my horror, that while Stephanie and I were up there exchanging vows, someone had broken into the pastor's office and robbed us.

So much for happily ever after.

●●●

This actually ended up being a good thing, because we all envision marriage as perfect but we all have a different definition of what perfect is. I quickly learned this on our honeymoon.

In the mid-90s the Puerto Rico board of tourism did a bang-up job on the commercials. They showed this couple looking over a cliff at a sparkling blue ocean view. The couple then looked at the camera and yelled, "Puerto Rico!"

It seemed perfect. So Stephanie and I both wanted to go there for our honeymoon. What they didn't tell you in that commercial was how hot Puerto Rico was in June. The commercial also showed a beautiful Spanish fort. This fort, El Morro, really looked like it was incredible. It was also closed on Mondays.

While Stephanie and I both thought Puerto Rico would be perfect, it was for different reasons. I wanted to see the sights; Stephanie wanted to hang out at the pool. I tried to hang at the pool as long as I could, but then I got antsy. So, against Stephanie's wishes, we went to El Morro on the Monday after we were married.

It was closed.

If I had stopped there, we might've been fine. We even asked a local about it. Her response should've clued me in. "Have you ever seen a Spanish fort? Anywhere on the East Coast of the US? Then you've seen this one."

Stephanie and I on our honeymoon, trying to find El Morro

I wasn't buying it. So I dragged poor Stephanie away from the pool for a second day, and we saw El Morro the next day. It was just OK. Definitely not perfect.

I think the key to being married is to leave your expectations at the door. When the groom carries the bride across the threshold, and you begin your life together, forget about perfect. Of course, I forgot to do the threshold thing because I was so mad about getting robbed, so it was easy for me.

We are inundated with images of what love is supposed to look like. Romantic dinners, walks on the beach together, holding hands while taking in a sunset. Stephanie and I have had moments like that, and I cherish them every time they come up.

But if marriage is a way to fullness in the Christian life, like theologian Thomas Merton said, then what is the perfect image of marital love?

I'd start with the image of a beaten, bleeding man on a cross.

People love to quote the apostle Paul and say that a wife is supposed to honor her husband. Some people take it even further, translating "honor" as "obey."

166

These same people fail to mention what Paul says about a husband, how he is expected to love his wife "as Christ loved the church." That kind of love blows way past honoring and obeying. It involves dying to yourself. It involves sacrifice.

I've learned marriage is not about give and take. It's not about meeting in the middle. It's about two people sacrificing, giving everything they have to the other person.

It is perhaps the most difficult thing a person could ever undertake. But it is also the most beautiful. I have learned so much and grown so much from the life I've built with Stephanie.

While we were dating, Stephanie and I saw a movie called (I think) *Singles*. In the film, the girl says she's fine with doing the cooking, but what she wants is a man who will do the dishes. It's a great analogy for the give and take of marriage. When Stephanie and I got married, we decided to take that analogy literally. More often than not she cooks, and more often than not I clean up. While I bristled a bit the first couple of times, I have come to enjoy the process. Except for the time I scrubbed a nonstick pan with a Brillo pad. Apparently that's not a combination that is meant to happen.

But although a lot of people say marriage is about give and take, and I might have even been guilty of saying that myself, I don't think that's what marriage is all about. It's not give and take. It's give, and give, and give again.

One time an act of generosity ended in a hospital trip for Stephanie. We had just hosted the Third Day band Christmas party at our apartment, and had a great time. Stephanie had made this delicious pecan pie that was a big hit at the party. Afterward, she was standing in the kitchen preparing to do the dishes. She was cutting up the leftover pie, and I assumed a position at one of the barstools at the counter. We talked about the party and how everyone was doing.

At one point she was trying to drive a point home by waving her knife in the air. Something flung from the knife and landed on my shirt. Apparently it was blood; Stephanie had cut herself on the knife. Next thing we know we're at the emergency room.

So she cooks. I do the dishes.

My friend Pete Hixson, a pastor in Ohio, has described this whole idea of what perfect really looks like with a beautiful analogy: when we get married, our vows for each other are chiseled in stone. Everything else, all the little agreements, are written in pencil. Whenever we have a disagreement on the little things, we can pull out the eraser. But the big things are always there, always set in stone.

A funny thing happens when you give up on give and take and just give. You both change for the better.

If you both give out of your strengths, and look past each other's weaknesses, the marriage takes on a life of its own. It really is like two people becoming one.

It's never been perfect. But there have been moments when our marriage has been pretty close.

14

GETTING TO WHERE WE NEED TO BE

We can't come up with a dream too big for God, and he has given us every reason to believe he wants us to raise our level of expectation.

Chip Ingram, *Good to Great in God's Eyes*

Dreams are a big deal to God. Sometimes he uses them to communicate with people. He used a dream to tell Jacob that he would father a great nation. Joseph dreamed that God would make him ruler over Egypt, and it happened.

When we only dream for ourselves, our dreams often end up being small and selfish. Dreams work best when they're part of God's big picture. And I'm thankful that God's dream for us is usually bigger than what we dream for ourselves.

The happily ever after we dream for ourselves is narrow and one-dimensional. The road God takes us on often involves unforeseen twists and turns, but we always end up in a place that's thrilling and unexpected. Even the turns that feel like dead ends at the time—God can use those as well.

If you had asked me anytime from about 1991 to 1995 what my dream was, it went something like this: Third Day would leave Atlanta, loading up in a little van and pulling all our gear in a trailer. We'd drive for fifteen hours and do a show somewhere far away like upstate New York, performing for maybe a hundred people. We might do two shows while we were out, maybe three. Then we would turn around and drive all the way back home. We would do this full-time. I thought this was the coolest idea in the world. This is what I wanted to do. That was my end-all, be-all dream for my life. My happily ever after.

By the middle of 1995 we were a full-time touring band. By my 1991 standards, we had made it.

But God had bigger plans for Third Day. We did do the van thing for a while, but by late 1996 we were traveling in a bus on our own headlining tour. In 1999 we released *Time*. The first track on that record, "I've Always Loved You," got significant radio airplay. We decided to follow up *Time* with the *Offerings* album. We approached that recording almost as a throwaway record. We only wrote about three new songs for the project, recording those along with two cover songs over the course of about a week, then rounding out the album with some live tracks we had recorded while on tour the year before. *Offerings* has ended up being our biggest album to date. By 2001, our ten-year "overnight success story" was pretty much complete.

When you dream small and reach those goals, you get restless. The road looks straight, like it will always be the same. But fortunately God sees around the curves in the road.

Capturing a great onstage moment with the crowd

After working on music with Third Day, I started to realize that my musical MO I'd used since high school, the way I had jammed on music and came up with new ideas, pointed to something more. I realized that I was actually writing songs, and it was something I was good at and really enjoyed doing.

On our first couple of albums I would present some of my musical ideas to the rest of the band and we would work them up into songs. By our third album I began to write lyrics as well. Mac, Tai, and Brad were also working on songs of their own. It was a great creative season in the band as we would feed off of each other during the songwriting and then get together to make demos. We would do fairly elaborate overdubs on these demos, almost as if they were full records in themselves. This process culminated in our *Time* album, which still stands as one of my favorite records we've ever done.

● ● ●

Pastor Wayne Cordeiro talks about people in our lives called "dream releasers." These people help us take our dreams from the realm of talking and "just thinking about it" into the world of reality. Stephanie has filled that role in my life countless times.

One of the amazing things about Stephanie is that she sees things in me and believes in me even when I don't believe in myself. She saw my interest in writing songs and encouraged me to work past my procrastination by giving me a deadline of writing one song per month. I actually kept up that pace for many years.

Performing for the troops on our USO tour

It's nothing to call home about for a professional songwriter, but for a guy in a band who's traveling all the time it's not bad.

One night Stephanie and I were riding the MARTA train back from downtown Atlanta. We had been at a concert, and while I had been watching the show, Stephanie had been watching my reaction. And her wheels were turning.

"I've been thinking. You write really good songs. I think you should go to Nashville and write when you're not on the road," she said.

And so I started traveling up to Nashville during gaps in my schedule. Third Day's music publisher was very supportive of what I wanted to do. I met a lot of other great writers and started writing songs with them. While my initial desire was to write country songs, God always seemed to open doors for me in Christian music.

By 2001 I found myself in Nashville almost as much as I was in Atlanta, and Stephanie and I decided to make the leap and move to Nashville.

172

So we bought a home there. It was crazy how all of the little things we had struggled with in Atlanta came so easily for us in Nashville. We were invited to go to church with a friend of mine from another band, a church we loved instantly. I had been praying about somewhere that Stephanie would be comfortable with when I was gone. We joined a small group at the church with a few other couples, and she had a great circle of support whenever I was on the road. Also there was just this great sense of community among artists in Nashville that carried over to their spouses as well. It just felt right.

I had also been praying for a mentor in my life, someone who could speak into what I was doing, first as a Christian but also as a husband and a musician. The first Sunday we visited church, I was invited to go to a new mentoring group that was started by Randy, the worship pastor at the church.

But a funny thing happens when you move to a different city and everything is going well. Everything you do feels like it's part of the plan. I moved to Nashville to be a songwriter. I'm currently at the grocery store. Awesome! Grocery shopping is helping my music career. Getting the oil changed in my car? I'm hanging at the service station in service of my songwriting.

My pastor, David Eldridge, has talked about the danger of looking for God in the circumstances. It can work great in hindsight as a confirmation, but if you're trying to make decisions that way, good luck. You're just going to drive yourself crazy. And that's what I think I did about our move to Nashville. Was it really meant to be?

One week our Sunday school class did this exercise where we committed our plans to God. We were given little rocks and asked to write our dreams on them, then pray about it and put our rocks in the middle of the room. It was to symbolize

With Matthew West

our letting go of our dreams and letting God take over. Stephanie and I prayed about it and wrote a single word on our rock: *Nashville*. I went to put the rock in the middle of the room. Before I put it down, I looked down at the other rocks. At least five of them said *Nashville*.

Was Nashville just a popular place? Or was I dreaming a crowded and popular dream?

In hindsight, I was overthinking it, which is the problem when you try to look for God in the circumstances.

I really hoped that a big break would happen with my songwriting that would confirm our decision. While I got a few small to medium-sized breaks, nothing major or obvious happened.

I wrote a song with Matthew West and Steve Hindalong that wound up on a Christmas album. I wrote a song with my friend Marc Byrd that became the title track of the *Strong Tower* record for Kutless.

Then one week I heard from a writer friend of mine that a Big Time Country Band had agreed to listen to one of our songs. I figured that pretty soon I'd get a call telling me that Big Time Country Band had loved our track and wanted to record it. That call never came.

So, for five years, we lived in Nashville. I don't regret a single minute of it. We had some of the best times of our life while living there and made some of our dearest friends. I got plugged into a great mentoring group, and our small group at church really helped us through that time. So while I never really got an obvious confirmation that living in Nashville was what we were supposed to be doing, God used that time for good.

● ● ●

Around this time we did a show at Magic Kingdom out in California. This is the amusement park where KISS filmed *KISS Meets the Phantom of the Park*, one of my favorite films as a kid. It's also the place where Spinal Tap embarks on their "freeform jazz exploration" when they open up for the puppet show.

Partly due to being at this venue, and partly due to our goofy travel schedule that morning, Third Day was in a rather giddy mood—that point where you're beyond exhausted but so tired you can't actually sleep.

I held a bottle of water in my hand. Trying to shake things up, and perhaps get a laugh out of the other guys, I asked an innocent question. "Y'all want me to pour this water over my head?"

"Yes. Yes we do," came the response.

With that frame of mind (and my wet head) we walked around the amusement park and pondered the events of the previous night. We had just won five Dove Awards, including Artist of the Year. The Doves are like gospel music's answer to the Grammys. It was surreal. Several other artists had gathered backstage to prepare for the final song, so after we won we were congratulated by what felt like a Who's Who of Christian music.

Up to that point we had always thought of ourselves as outsiders in Christian music. While most other artists moved to Nashville when they signed to record companies, we had decided to stay put in Atlanta. Well, everyone except me.

And before this year, we had never really had any kind of good performance slot at the Doves. We were a Southern rock band, not part of the mainstream. And we were OK with that.

As we talked about it, we realized we no longer fit into the narrative we'd built for ourselves. If we won five Dove Awards, including Artist of the Year, we weren't on the outside anymore. What did this mean, if anything, in the grand scheme of things? And what were we supposed to do about it?

We didn't have a great answer that day. But it was another moment where the road curved for me, and God showed me again that his dream for Third Day and his dream for us individually was a little bit bigger than what we had for ourselves.

Not long after that, Bono visited Nashville. He shared with Tai and me and several other Christian artists about the AIDS crisis in southern Africa, and how this was a unique point in time where we could raise our voices and help make a difference.

Also during this time, a guy named Hugh Hewitt spoke at a conference my friend and mentor Randy put on. Hugh talked about "using your platform," and I was intrigued. I had heard the term *platform* used by authors who were wanting to expand their reach, but had never heard it mentioned in such a broad sense.

Did I have a platform?

All of these things culminated when Stephanie, Tai, and I traveled to South Africa with Habitat for Humanity in 2002. While we were there to help build houses, we heard stories about the AIDS pandemic and how it was affecting so many people in that region.

Through many conversations with the other guys and with Nigel, our tour pastor, it hit home for me that yes, we had a platform in Third Day, and God wanted us to use that platform to point to worthy causes and people who were doing great things around the world. Besides Habitat for Humanity, we've also worked with World Vision and Food for the Hungry concerning the issue of child poverty around the world. Brad, Tai, and I also traveled to Lesotho in southern Africa in 2004.

Backstage with Max Lucado on the Come Together and Worship tour

Rocking out with Steven Curtis Chapman on the SCC3D tour (Photo credit: William Barber)

I have come to believe that it's not just authors or people in rock bands who have a platform. It's everybody. We all have a sphere of influence. If you're a teacher, God wants to use you in exactly the place you are to reach those people he has placed in your life. You are able to impact people that folks like me will never be able to get close to.

I like this idea of a platform because it involves stewardship. While we can work on it and use it and expand it, ultimately a platform is not something we create on our own. It's something God entrusts us with. We act as stewards, using what we've been given to hopefully bring God glory.

The Prayer of Jabez was such a popular book in part because it hit on this fundamental truth. God has given us all a platform, and if we are good stewards of it, he will bless it and expand it. But it's all for God's glory, not ours.

This idea of stewardship gives the control back to God, where it rightfully belongs. And what a relief that is. We don't have to worry about the future, about this happily ever after business, because God's got it. That is a very freeing place to live from.

I have learned that the road God has us on is not a smooth one. There are curves. Some of those are caused by decisions we make and some are caused by circumstances beyond our control. But it is not our job to try to figure those things out. God wants to use us right where we are.

15

HANGING ON AND LETTING GO

Everything is safe which we commit to Him, and nothing is really safe which is not so committed.

A. W. Tozer, *The Pursuit of God*

I have always said that I would throw out this little bit of advice if I ever got the chance. This might be as good of a chance as I'll ever get. Would-be Dads, take note: if your child is ever born by C-section, there's something they should tell you but they don't.

Stephanie and I visited the doctor several times during her first pregnancy, and everything was routine. But when we went in about a week before the birth, our doctor changed her tune quite a bit. Stephanie was great with child and she is kind of a small person.

"Are you guys set on a traditional birth? Because if you are, there are some things I might need to tell you," the doctor said.

Then she launched into little details like the possibility of having to break our daughter's shoulder to get her out of the birth canal. I swooned a bit and then sat down in the nearest chair I could find. The doctor was cool. She didn't even seem to mind that I took the neat little swiveling chair and made her sit in the awkward chair with the arms in the wrong places.

We reminded the doctor that we had sort of been rooting for a C-section the whole time. Then we came up with a plan. This was going down the next Tuesday. We were going to check into the hospital at around 6:00 a.m., and a couple hours later we were going to have a little bundle of joy.

With the small exception of the 6:00 a.m. part, this sounded perfect. When Tuesday morning came, we loaded up the car and drove down to the hospital. Different nurses and doctors came in and got Stephanie ready for the procedure. I did my best to do the dad thing, asking questions at the right time but mostly staying out of the way, holding Stephanie's hand, things like that.

Right before Abbie was born—the moment I grew up

There's just one little detail nobody told me about.

They put Stephanie on one of those gurney things then wheeled her into an elevator and took her to another floor. I walked beside her. My pride and excitement of entering into this parenting world were now replaced by another emotion. I was suppressing

180

it, but I knew it from years of doing shows. Unlike the normal stage fright I get before a lot of shows, this was straight-up terror. I kept smiling, trying to maintain my poker face, but I'm pretty sure nobody was buying it.

"You OK, Dad?" One of the nurses asked me right before we walked through the big, serious double doors leading to the operating room.

"Doing great!"

"OK. While they're getting Mom ready, you're going to need to follow me."

Here's where my bit of advice comes in. You see, whenever they do a C-section, they leave the dad outside to wait while they get everything ready for the surgery. Totally routine. I get it. But the thing is, when you're in the throes of that weird hospital-childbirth thing, it doesn't feel routine at all. It feels like something's wrong. And time plays that funny trick on you where it decides to pack an eternity into each passing second.

Don't say I didn't warn you.

I thought it would be a minute or two. Then it turned into ten, then began to approach twenty. What had happened was our doctor got held up in traffic on the way to the hospital that morning and was about twenty minutes late getting to the OR. So I was sitting outside the operating room, by myself, just a barrel of nerves, for the better part of those twenty minutes. Again, no big deal. Totally routine. But it didn't feel that way at all.

I've had a few moments in my life that seemed to tear my life into sections, like the unfortunate doughnut/truck incident all those years ago, when I was able to pack what seems like a lifetime of memories into one little flash. I was a different person for having gone through the process.

181

I thought back over the whirlwind my life had been over the last decade or so, and how Stephanie had sort of put her dreams on hold to help me fulfill mine. And how we were about to begin this new chapter together.

Now, if I really think about it, I can see that this was the moment, finally, at age thirty, when I grew up.

After eons went by, the nice nurse came back.

"OK, Dad. You ready?"

"Sure!" I somehow managed to croak.

The truth is, I wasn't ready. I was the youngest child in my family and I was too young to really remember being around any younger cousins. When I was older, I avoided infants whenever possible. I had no idea what I was getting into.

As I walked back toward the operating room, I prayed one of the most honest prayers a man can ever come up with: "God, help me."

⬤ ⬤ ⬤

They did finally let me in there. Everything went off without a hitch. After cleaning up our daughter, Abbie, they propped her up on Stephanie. We got a picture together. I'll be honest, I didn't really know what I was supposed to do. The nurse, sensing this, said, "You can hold her hand if you want."

I held out my hand, my finger really, and the most amazing thing happened. This tiny little hand grabbed mine. It was like sweet baby Abbie was saying to me, "It's OK, Daddy. You don't have to know everything. We'll figure this out together. You just have to be my daddy."

I remember riding in airplanes as a kid. It was the most fun thing in the world. I'd sit in my seat and look out the window at the clouds and the landscape. Then the nice flight attendants would bring me snacks and drinks. One of my favorite parts was when we would hit turbulence. It felt like I was riding on a roller coaster in the sky.

Nowadays I have absolutely no point of contact with those thoughts. I have grown to tolerate flying out of necessity. I'm not sure how I would pull off the travel thing without

Holding newborn Abbie on the day of her baby dedication

being able to go home again, and flying makes that a ton easier. Fun? Not so much.

For a while there, when I was in my twenties, I would get pretty freaked out on planes. And I think a lot of that had to do with the fact that I was a grown-up. You see, when I was a kid, the pilot represented a grown-up and therefore had everything all figured out. So of course he or she knew how to operate a plane safely. Then when I was a grown-up myself I realized that not only did I not know everything but I was still kind of a little kid on the inside. So, if I was that way, it only stood to reason that the pilot was that way too. Knowing what an idiot I was capable of being so much of the time, was I really expected to place my life in the hands of another potential idiot like myself?

You see, they weren't just letting me hold my child. They were putting me in charge of carrying her down to our hospital room while they finished up with Stephanie.

I figured they would put a nurse in charge of that one, and kind of let me ease into this dad thing.

183

A nurse did accompany me, at least. We got on the elevator to go down to our floor. She smiled at me. I thought she was laughing about this new dad freak-out I was having, but I guess I played it pretty well.

"Have you looked at her toes yet? Which one of y'all do you think she got her toes from?" she asked.

Oh, I get it. They're way more focused on this new human just brought into the world than they are the thirty-year-old holding her. Maybe I can *pull this off.*

The doors to the elevator opened to an image that will be ingrained in my head for as long as I live. Both sets of grandparents were standing there, beaming. I guess somebody had told them where to wait to be able to see baby Abbie.

As the grandmas oohed and aahed over their first granddaughter, I had a similar realization to the one I had in my high school stadium bleachers all those years ago: *It's going to be OK, because I have all these people around me I can lean on.*

That was when I became a grown-up. For others it might be different, but for me the realization that God had put me in charge of another life, another soul, made me want to be the best daddy I could be.

I wore one of my dad's shirts that day. A few months prior, we had cleaned out a closet at the house I grew up in and found a bunch of Dad's clothes. I had taken a couple of his shirts as keepsakes. It seemed right that, if he couldn't be there, he should somehow be represented.

I had also found the little bear he had given me in the hospital when I was born and placed it in Abbie's hospital crib. In the newborn pictures of Abbie we emailed to family and friends, you could see that little bear.

Later that day, Stephanie left the room with a nurse and it was just me and Abbie in there. I held Abbie up against my shoulder and walked over to a mirror. All I could do was laugh at myself. Me? A dad? But it made perfect sense.

Abbie began to stir and whimper a little bit.

I rocked back and forth, bouncing her gently against my shoulder.

"Not gonna cry. No, no, no." I said that over again and again, making a little song out of it. Then, in the same rhythm as the little song, I shushed her.

And Abbie fell asleep.

●●●

It is amazing what being a parent does for your sense of perspective. People often talk about having a new understanding of God because you can relate to him as a parent. I got a small sense of that, but it was mainly lost in this new sense of urgency. I felt this definite, intense responsibility for someone other than myself. There was now this little life who totally relied on Stephanie and me for, well, everything.

Maybe I was taking things a little too far, but I didn't care.

From that moment on I jumped into the daddy thing with both feet. I read books on parenting. I drove carefully. I helped with diapers, with nighttime feedings. All the little dad things you're supposed to do, I did those.

A few years later we had our second daughter, Kitty. I did a little better this time around when it came time to wait outside for the surgery to start. Other than that, the dad pressure only intensified. This time I even started watching my weight. I wore my seat belt all the time. I wanted to be around when my kids were grown-up.

●●●

They say a good thing is a good thing—until it's not.

If you've ever been to the Florida Keys, you know that by car there is basically only one way in and one way out. Therefore you have to plan some extra time whenever you have somewhere you have to be. Despite allowing myself some buffer time, I was anxious as I drove my family from Hawks Cay to the Miami airport. We had been down there for spring break and had just enjoyed a wonderful, carefree week in the sun. Now it was time to head back to reality. A long drive, the returning of a rental car, and a flight, all with children, loomed in my future, and the happily ever after of home seemed far off. It was safe to say I was a little stressed.

We left our hotel promptly at 9:00 a.m. Not being very familiar with the area, I promised my family that we'd stop at "the first place we saw" to get breakfast. The "first place we saw" ended up being a McDonald's exactly ninety-one minutes later.

This was before the era of the McDonald's all-day breakfast. If you're doing the math along with me, you know that ninety-one minutes later puts us at 10:31 a.m. At McDonald's back then, that was a formula for trouble.

On a side note, I still for the life of me can't figure out who would want to eat a hamburger at 10:31 in the morning. I get the whole changeover thing. But why in the world couldn't they do a slow fade between 10:30 and 11? I guess McDonald's isn't run by musicians. But I digress. You are here to sit in on the low point of my parenting career. So we pull into the drive-thru at 10:31.

I humored myself: "You guys still serving breakfast?" I asked.

Hey—you have not because you ask not, right? And the lady on the other side of the speaker gave me the faintest glimmer of hope.

"All we got left is a McGriddle, an Egg McMuffin, and a sausage and cheese biscuit."

"Great. I'll take them all."

I felt like I had just dodged a bullet. It wasn't perfect, but we were getting breakfast and we were going to make it to the airport without a hitch. My wife took Kitty, our youngest daughter, inside to change a diaper, and I stayed in the car with Abbie, our six-year-old.

"OK, baby. Here's a sausage and cheese biscuit."

"I don't want a sausage and cheese biscuit. I want a regular biscuit."

"OK, I can fix that. Check this out," I said, pulling off the sausage along with most of the cheese. I handed Abbie the biscuit, proud of the way dads can sometimes look like they're doing magic to their kids.

Tears welled up in Abbie's eyes. She wasn't buying it. "This still has cheese on it."

Now, bear in mind, I was not angry at this point in time. Frazzled even sounds a bit strong. I would describe myself as maybe a bit harried. Over the next 1.6 seconds, I mulled over how to respond. I was torn between two harsh ways to say "Eat your biscuit." Somewhere in the vocal sector of my brain, a synapse must have misfired, because what came out was something different and entirely unexpected. If it had been a sitcom, they would have bleeped it out. If it were live television, I would have been slapped with a fine. These words were the absolute last thing a parent wants to say to their six-year-old child.

I'm still trying to recover from that one.

One time one of Abbie's friends from school spent the night. For the first couple of hours, the girls played, showing off their cheerleading and tumbling routines. Then we took them up the hill to watch a Mardi Gras parade. There were floats and costumes and beads. The kids loved it. Then we took them to get frozen yogurt. As we were walking into the yogurt place I heard thunder overhead, but didn't think much of it. Then, as we began walking back down the hill toward home, storm sirens started blaring. The kids tensed up.

My girls and I, 2016

"Daddy, is it a tornado?"

"I don't think so, sweetie. It's just a bad storm. Let's walk on back, though."

As we were walking home, we passed a house where some guys were sitting out on their porch.

"Kids, you better get on home," one of them said with a laugh. "Tornado's coming."

Thanks, man. There goes my attempt at sheltering sensitive ears.

And maybe that's the problem. Try as you might, you can't shelter your children from everything. It will make you crazy. And crazy is not a great place to try to parent from.

There's a phenomenon in our family called "grumpy dad syndrome," or GDS for short. It's when I focus so much on my role as a father that I forget to be Daddy.

GDS reared its head in New York City a few years ago when we were trying to find somewhere to eat at 10:00 p.m. Now, there are a gazillion restaurants in New York, I know, but our hotel was in a business district and everything shut down

188

after dark. We walked and looked and asked and walked and looked and finally found a little Italian place. I was so relieved that we found it that I guess I just sort of clammed up when we sat down. After our food came and we ate, Stephanie told me she was going to take the kids back to the hotel so I could have some time to pull it back together. What?

It happened another time when I came home from a run of shows, and we decided to take the kids to a local steak place for a special dinner. I had a great time. I was aware of being tired from travel, but I felt like everything was fine. Except Kitty was excited that I was home and felt the need to climb on me in the booth. Later she told Mommy that I had been grumpy that night.

And the problem is, even when I'm in the middle of it, that is the last thing in the world I want. I want to be there for my kids. I want them to have great memories from their early years. And I want to set the template for how men are supposed to treat them. Because, good Lord, let's face it, the male species hasn't done a very good PR job.

As in everything else involving my children, my heart is in the right place. I was just trying to make everything right and let their childhood be perfect, because mine was not. But I realized I was holding on so tightly to the happily ever after of security for my children that it was becoming a death grip on the idea of me being the dad my kids need me to be.

I have gotten a little better about it, but I have a long way to go.

● ● ●

Maybe it's that I need to let go. Or at least let go of my grip a little bit and give the reins to God.

189

Stephanie and I at the Grammys, 2003—this was the first year we won.

A. W. Tozer wrote a great little book called *The Pursuit of God*. I try to read it every couple of years. It's really inspiring, but there's one chapter in particular that challenges me in a major way.

It's called "The Blessedness of Possessing Nothing," and it does a beautiful job of relating the story of Abraham and Isaac with our view of possessions. Just as Abraham had to be willing to let go of Isaac, faith requires that we let go of everything we own. Anything that gets in between us and God should be placed on the altar of our lives.

That goes for relationships too. Even those we hold the most dear. For me, that means I need to let go of the myth of security. To think that I can shelter and protect my children from anything bad that might happen in this world is a flat-out lie. Instead, I need to give it over to God.

In return, God does an amazing thing. Just like the end of the book of Job, he gives everything back. But that stewardship idea comes into play again. I don't own anything—it's all God's. I am here to take care of what I've been entrusted with. And that especially includes my kids.

My church does a neat thing for birthdays. At the beginning of the month, the pastor will ask everyone who has a birthday in that month to stand up and say what they want.

It's not just a birthday thing. So many times people approach Jesus for a miracle, and he asks them pointedly, "What do you want?"

On my birthday one year, I said that I wanted my children to figure out their gifts and their place in the world. I know I won't always be there for them, and I want them to have landmarks in their life to guide their way when things get tough, just like I had.

Throwing down a little slide guitar

191

16

HOMESICK

"How would this do: and they all settled down and
lived together happily ever after?"

"It will do well, if it ever comes to that," said Frodo.

"Ah!" said Sam. "And where will they live? That's
what I often wonder."

J. R. R. Tolkien, *The Fellowship of the Ring*

It is one thing to write about things that happened so long
ago, when I was a kid. More recent memories are something else entirely.

Parker Palmer is an author I've recently discovered, and
he's rapidly becoming a favorite of mine. He talks about
a kind of perspective that can only come with age. It's an
ability to look back and "listen to your life." That is easier
to do when you're talking about distant memories. But what
about the more recent past?

I feel obligated to try. While those early experiences became part of the landmarks that have guided me through life, I continue to learn some very valuable lessons. Hopefully, the further along I go on this Hurt Road journey, the more God will teach me to let go of those little lies that get in the way of who he truly is and who he wants me to be.

This is painful for me to say, because I have blogged at length about finding home. Early versions of this book even referenced the concept. But more and more, this idea is being stripped away and revealing a deeper truth lying underneath.

I am learning that the concept of home is a myth.

By fall 2005 Stephanie and I had lived in Nashville for over four years and were quite happy. It was difficult at times, because I was still in the band and still had to go to Atlanta all the time.

But we had a church we loved. I was part of a mentoring group I loved. We were a loose-knit bunch of guys who would meet for breakfast every Tuesday and talk about our faith, what we'd been reading, and whatever other crazy ideas were floating around our heads. I had dreamed about being a part of a group like this for years.

We were also part of a small group and had a lot of really close friends. We were in a house we absolutely loved. We had only lived there for a couple of years, but there were already so many great memories. Most of all, this was the town where Abbie was born.

It felt like we had found something of our very own that wasn't tied in with family or me being in the band. We were finally building something that was ours.

We had moved to Nashville in search of an elusive happily ever after: the concept of home. After Abbie was born this feeling only intensified. But after a few years "home"

Abbie was so excited to be a big sister!

changed into something a little different.

One weekend we were visiting family in Atlanta. I had a show and we decided to stay in town for a couple of days because it was Stephanie's mom's birthday. That whole trip I kept thinking about how much harder it was to leave every time. How we'd have dinner with family and I would already sort of be counting the time down until we wouldn't see them again, kind of like that clock that clouds my memories of Dad. It was always bittersweet.

I was starting to wonder if maybe we needed to move back to Atlanta. But I wasn't going to bring it up. Maybe the next time Steph and I were having some kind of candid conversation I could mention it, but not now. Things seemed to be going smoothly.

When we got in the car—before we even left the parking lot—Stephanie said, "There's something I've been thinking a lot about lately. Don't kill me, but I think we need to move back here."

I don't know if Stephanie senses what's weighing on me or if it's the other way around. Or maybe God is literally working on us both at the same time. Whatever it is, it's pretty incredible.

We knew we couldn't move back right away, but our wheels were set in motion. We decided we'd start getting our house ready to sell and would put it on the market the following spring. From that moment forward, we were spending less time in Nashville and more in Atlanta. Our move was a heart one before it became a physical one.

● ● ●

Kitty, our younger daughter, used to do this thing when she was little that got me every time. We had just moved into a new house but hadn't really gotten settled in yet. Kitty would get tired or hungry and start doing that whiny thing that little kids do. And what she said just broke my heart: "Daddy, I want to go home."

I know what Kitty meant. She was tired and over it, and she wanted to go to the place that brought her peace. I don't think it's only little kids, either. We all have a place like that.

For me, it is a place that doesn't really exist anymore. The first house I lived in is still there, but my dad's prediction all those years ago came true: the neighborhood has changed so much since I lived there that it has become totally unrecognizable.

Even though it's not there, I still look for home. If I can't find it, I'll build it.

We moved from Nashville back to Atlanta because we were looking for home. Stephanie's dad and brother built us a beautiful house. When our kids were old enough to go to school, we sent them to a private Christian school.

Everything seemed perfect. Until it wasn't.

When the economy shifted in 2008, people's buying habits changed. It felt like we woke up one morning and everybody had stopped buying CDs. The music industry shifted from selling CDs to selling concert tickets. The stability we thought we had just wasn't there anymore. Stephanie and I saw the writing on the wall. This house we'd built, and the lifestyle we'd built alongside it, were just not sustainable.

So a few years ago we moved to Woodstock. It's only a few miles up the road, and really only a thirty-minute drive. We definitely wanted to keep our kids in the same school, which was almost right across the street from where we had lived before.

Woodstock was a cool little town and ours was a cool house. You could walk out our door and up a hill and be in this neat little shopping and dining district. The house was a bit small compared to where we had been before, but so what if it didn't have any storage? We could get a storage unit somewhere. So what if there wasn't really a yard? So what if it was far from the kids' school?

Kitty loved the house instantly. Instead of a yard, we had a little side area out the back of the kitchen. You actually had to walk through this area to get to our garage. But Kitty loved playing in this area. Instead of grass it was filled with this pebbly aggregate stuff. Kitty would come home from preschool and play in the pebbles.

Abbie was in a different place. Or rather, she didn't have a place. She was at that stage where she needed friends to play with. There was only one other girl her age in our neighborhood. Abbie would go play with her sometimes after school. Abbie also needed somewhere to play. So that involved me walking with her about a quarter mile up the hill toward downtown where there was this little playground area.

But the worst was driving to school. I did a test drive before we bought the house, but I was thinking with my heart, not my head. On good days it would take me thirty-five minutes to get to their school. And then forty minutes to get home. I got to do that again at lunchtime to pick Kitty up from

Kitty and I leading worship at her preschool's chapel service

preschool, and then once more for good measure at 3:00 for Abbie.

It wasn't all a nightmare. I did get to spend a lot of time with the girls in the car. We would listen to music together, and I would put together different little mix tapes like "Abbie 2012" and "Abbie Kitty Zig Zag." We still listen to "Abbie Kitty Zig Zag" to this day.

Kitty was having that one year that all kids, at least mine, seem to go through, where they decide they love Christmas but haven't gotten the memo that it just happens in December. She was trying to make the idea of keeping the Christmas spirit going year round a literal one. So for months we would listen to Christmas music, and Alvin and the Chipmunks Christmas music in particular, just about nonstop in the car. It was fun to have that.

The last straw came for Stephanie pretty much the first time she had to make that drive. It took me a couple of more months. Maybe I didn't want to admit I'd made a mistake. Or maybe it was just that I really did love that house. I still do. But I held out for a few months. Then one day the traffic was especially wretched. Like a good soldier I made the almost-hour trek to the kids' school and I almost even got them there on time. Then I turned around and sat in all that traffic again. I had left home about seven, and now I finally got home around nine. I was like Axl Rose singing "Mr.

197

Brownstone," only instead of being in bed till 9, I had spent all that time in the car.

I walked in the door, exhausted. Greeting me, right in the middle of the kitchen counter, was Kitty's lunch. Apparently I would be making four long car trips that day.

I wish I could tell you that Stephanie and I were synced up in our frustration and readiness to move. But it didn't quite work out that way. We were on the way to meet a friend for lunch down in Smyrna (more time in the car!) and Stephanie got really quiet. I could tell she was thinking about something.

"Don't freak out, but I think we need to move back closer to the school," she said at last. "I'm not saying we have to do it right now or anything. I'm just saying I think it needs to happen."

Despite her pleas to the contrary, I pretty well freaked out. I had felt this low to medium level of stress for a few years, since we had decided to move back to Atlanta. But it had felt like such a "God thing." Why wasn't it happening?

●●●

I have found in my short time on this planet that often my stress happens when I try to take things upon myself instead of letting God be in control. This time I took a breath and tried to let God do his thing.

I was pretty amazed by the result.

That summer, probably about a month after our fun little conversation in the car, we got a note in the mailbox. It was from a couple saying that they really liked our neighborhood and our street in particular. They would be extremely interested in talking to us about buying our house.

It sounded like a scam. At first we just laughed at it.

But then, a week or so later, we sat out on the front porch, talking about how we probably were going to need to move, and sooner rather than later. I was definitely on board by this time. Stephanie's face lit up.

"Why don't we just call those people? The ones who put the note in the mailbox? I mean the worst thing that's going to happen is we're going to find out they already bought a house or they changed their mind."

I agreed that while it wasn't a great idea, it was certainly harmless. So Stephanie called them. I was out touring. Ironically—or not—this was the run of shows that included the time we met a couple in New Jersey who inspired the song "I Need a Miracle" and would provide the title for our *Miracle* album.

I called home from Detroit. I have many memories of calling home from that same venue. They always seem to happen when we're making big decisions like this. We did a photo shoot in about the same place where I usually stroll around talking on the phone. So, as you're reading this, if you can look at the inside of the *Lead Us Back* album, you'll see the general spot I'm talking about. If you're a visual person, that is.

Stephanie said that it was actually a nice couple, some empty nesters who lived not far away but just wanted to live closer to their friends. They hung out a lot in the downtown area at the top of the hill and were intrigued by the idea of living right there and being able to walk home. The way they talked about our neighborhood almost made me want to buy our house again, let alone sell it.

The wife came by and looked at it, then the husband. By that Monday night they were making an offer on our house.

Now we were under the gun. Where would we move to?

● ● ●

We looked in a couple of neighborhoods near the school, and even found a couple of houses we liked. There was one we decided would be the one to beat. If we couldn't find anything else in the next few days, we were going to make a move on that one.

One night, as we were getting ready to go to bed, Stephanie asked if I remembered the "Facebook house."

Not long before, maybe a couple of months prior, Stephanie had found, oddly enough, a house that was listed for sale in a Facebook post. She had even shown it to me, and we both agreed it was perfect. It even had a wall in one of the kids' rooms with a Georgia Tech logo painted on it.

We went back and tried to find the page. Apparently the people had taken it down. We assumed that, because we couldn't find it, it must have sold. We couldn't imagine an awesome house like that still being on the market. But my wife has proven to be persistent over the years, and this was definitely one of those cases. She picked up the phone and called friends until she located someone who knew the couple who had posted that house.

Come to find out, the owners had just taken down the Facebook post about it because the only responses they seemed to have gotten were from friends wondering why they'd moved. The house was still there, still cute as a button. And it was still for sale.

The next day we drove out to the house and took a look at it. The wife greeted us at the door and explained how excited she was for us to come and look, and if nothing else, she could share with us a little bit about how Third Day was part of their story.

We had taken the girls with us because it was summer and we didn't have anything else to do. We went upstairs and looked at the kids' rooms and they loved them. Something about the way the ceilings sloped gave it sort of a farmhouse feel. I was taken back to that Thanksgiving at my aunt's house in Elberton, in a way. In one of the girls' rooms Kitty even found a toy horse to play with. Something about that warmed my heart and broke it at the same time. That bittersweet confusion of moving. The joy, the sadness, the sense of transience that it brings about, that sense of mortality, somehow all seemed to me to be wrapped up in that little horse.

As we walked around, looking at room after room—falling more in love with the house yet trying to play it cool with the owner and with each other—she shared a little bit about their story. Her husband was a doctor and had recently felt a pull toward the mission field. Doctors are very scarce in Africa, and he had found a great organization that brought doctors over to help fulfill that deep need. And as it turns out, he had initially felt drawn to this idea from a speaker at a Third Day show many years before.

● ● ●

Through this process I have learned that it doesn't really matter how many times you move. There is a restlessness you just can't escape. And you can move to a new location but that doesn't mean you'll leave your problems behind. Wherever you go, there you are.

Switchfoot did a song called "This Is Home" for *The Chronicles of Narnia: Prince Caspian* sound track several years ago. It's my favorite song of theirs—and one of my favorite songs of all time. I think they tap into this restlessness thing better than anybody.

Singing "Freebird" on a little plane during the Lead Us Back tour

We're restless because the happily ever after of home during this life is a myth. Jesus didn't have a home on earth. Remember, "the Son of Man has no place to lay his head" (Matt. 8:20). If Jesus didn't have a home, why should I expect to have one? I shouldn't.

Heaven is home.

That simple shift in perspective can get you thinking out of a different place: not your temporal, earthly home, but your eternal, heavenly home. It makes you want different things. People become more important than possessions. And above all, God is in control.

When we bought the house we're living in now, the family changed their "For Sale" sign to read something a little unusual. But I think they had a pretty good handle on where home really is and who's really in control. Instead of "For Sale," the sign now read, "He Owns It All."

17

GOD BLESS ME

What God longs to teach us is that when we have nothing left but God, God is enough.

Dan DeHaan, *The God You Can Know*

I was well into my thirties before I recognized perhaps the most dangerous happily ever after myth of all. I didn't identify it at first because it's so subtle. Also, I think on some subconscious level, a lot of us think it's true.

The myth goes something like this: if I am obedient to God, then he will bless me with a great life.

There are many Bible verses that almost say this. John 10:10 is probably quoted the most: "I have come that they may have life, and have it to the full."

We can also look to several stories in Scripture that seem to reflect this idea as well. After remaining obedient through many trials, Job was blessed twofold. Abraham was made the father of many nations. Joseph was a ruler over Egypt.

The good part of the story is that I experienced a genuine personal revival a few years back. It's not that I had given up on faith—it's more that I got comfortable. This revival would come from the most unlikely of places: one of my childhood heroes.

For my birthday a few years ago, Stephanie came up with the best surprise. She wouldn't tell me what it was, but she seemed really proud of it so I could tell it was something big. We got in the car, and she still wouldn't tell me where we were going—she would only tell me where to turn.

"OK, I know you hate surprises, so I don't want this to be ruined by your being surprised," she said. "I'll tell you what it is if you want to know."

"Let me see if I can figure it out."

I've always been a fan of guessing games, and drive her and the kids crazy trying to make a game or a song (or both) out of practically anything. After some questioning, I deduced that my birthday present wasn't exactly a thing. It was more of an event. I started getting a little worried. I didn't want this to be some awkward lunch with somebody I didn't know.

"Are we having lunch with somebody I don't know?"

Stephanie smiled. "Maybe."

"Is it somebody famous or something?"

"Maybe."

We kept this up as she navigated me onto I-285, the massive interstate that serves as the unofficial barrier between downtown Atlanta and its suburbs. If they'd had this road built a little earlier, Sherman might have got stuck in traffic and the city wouldn't have burnt down. But then we wouldn't get to be the Phoenix City, or whatever they call it.

I figured out that this mystery person was a sports figure of some sort and a personal favorite of mine. When I was a little kid I was a huge Falcons fan. I always liked the Braves too, but my fandom didn't reach fever pitch until I was in college. I went through a little basketball phase in high school, when Dominique Wilkins led the Hawks to the playoffs a couple of times. All of the posters of musicians I had on my wall in high school took up places that were previously held by basketball players. Could it be Dominique? Or Spud Webb?

Something about that didn't seem right. It had to be football, because I still loved football.

"Is it Steve Bartkowski?" I asked at last.

Steve Bartkowski quarterbacked the Falcons in the late '70s and early '80s. They had an amazing run in 1980 and were favored to go to the Super Bowl until they lost to Dallas in the playoffs. I remember nervously watching that game with my uncle. I had a little blue football that somebody had given me that I twirled nervously as I paced back and forth, watching the Falcons' big lead fade in the second half until the unthinkable happened and Danny White hit Drew Pearson on a long touchdown pass. I was seven years old. I cried.

I still hate the Cowboys.

"Maybe." Stephanie's devious smile was now a full-on grin. I knew I was probably right.

We eventually pulled into the parking lot of a restaurant. A couple of minutes later I was sitting at a table talking to Steve Bartkowski.

We ended up having a great lunch with Steve and his wife, Sandee. They are good people. For the first couple of minutes I did the thing where I'm trying to play it cool and think I'm doing OK. Then I realize my mouth is moving and I'm talking nonstop. This time I was telling Steve all about that 1980 season and how I felt that the 1981 team also had a lot of potential but were depleted by injuries and never really had a chance.

Steve was really gracious. "Yeah, we had a lot of injuries."

After I sort of calmed down a bit, we ended up having a great conversation. Steve talked about a lot of what he's been up to—he's been a successful businessman but is still on the board of the Falcons, so he still goes to all the games and is actively involved with the team. We talked about Matt Ryan and his natural ability to read a defense. We talked about Sandee and her art. Stephanie was running a children's boutique at the time and we talked about that too.

But I still didn't have my main question answered. I looked at Stephanie. "How in the world did you pull this together?"

It turned out that Stephanie had tried to track down an autographed jersey for my birthday. A simple Google search showed that Steve went through a booking agent whenever he did any speaking engagements, and we knew one of the guys at the agency. One phone call and she had Steve's email address. She emailed Steve to ask about getting a jersey signed. Steve wanted to take it to the next level and arrange a meeting.

It's amazing the things you can do if you try. It's also amazing to see how nice some people can be. Steve and Sandee are that kind of people.

After meeting Steve I had to post about it on my blog. A couple of people responded and asked if I'd read Steve's book. I didn't even know Steve had a book. I tracked it down on Amazon and read it. That book, *Intercepted by Christ*, absolutely changed my life. I would put it on the level of *A Wrinkle in Time* or the C. S. Lewis books I read as a kid for sheer amount of impact.

The title, *Intercepted by Christ*, sums up the book perfectly, not just in content but in the way it's laid out. It starts out as a normal biography, taking you through a chapter

Best birthday present ever! Meeting
Falcons legend Steve Bartkowski

about Steve growing up in California and then a chapter about Steve
playing for Cal and the adversity
he encountered there. Then, when
Steve gets to the NFL, he has a
couple of great seasons with the
Falcons and then gets benched
for a few games. June Jones, his
backup quarterback, tells Steve, "I
am going to quarterback this team
until you give your life to God."

It is at this point you realize that
this isn't a normal biography—it's
Steve's testimony. After Steve's life
gets "intercepted by Christ," so
does the book. And that's when things get really interesting.

The book's author, Dan DeHaan, was the Falcons' chap-
lain and a close friend of Steve's. Dan was a legendary figure
in both the sports world and in Atlanta's spiritual community.
He spoke regularly at Metro Bible Study for many years until
he died tragically in a plane accident. While his life was too
short, he left a long legacy. It is not a stretch to say that he
laid the foundation for what would later become the 7:22
Bible study, Northpoint Church, and the Passion movement.

Throughout the rest of *Intercepted by Christ*, Dan walks
through the discipleship process Bartkowski undertook after
becoming a Christian. In doing so, he leads the reader in a
study of the foundations of the Christian faith. It is a must-
read for anyone who wants to take their faith to the next level.

Intercepted by Christ was a big part of a major spiritual
breakthrough I had during this time. It wasn't that I was
struggling in my faith or had doubts or anything of that

nature. It's just that I was at a place of complacency. And because we had been so focused on all our moving around and getting settled for the last few years, my faith had just not really been a priority for a while.

My biggest takeaway from that book would have to be the visual of Dan going out into the wilderness. He and Steve were about to make a big decision, and Dan wanted to go spend time in the woods before committing to it. In his next book, *The God You Can Know*, Dan talks about going out into the woods in Michigan as a teenager, in the snow, and contemplating God. He would read a big systematic theology book and then walk out into the snow and sort of pray it through and ask God to reveal himself.

I read these books and wanted that kind of faith.

That visual has stuck with me: having a faith so strong that it makes you want to drop everything and get immersed in it like you would a wilderness. A faith so intimate that it makes you want to walk in the woods with God.

For the next several months, I prayed more than I had in my entire adult life. I would read Bible passages and, like Dan DeHaan, walk out into the woods and think about what they were saying to me.

I felt closer to God than I had perhaps ever felt.

So what was wrong with that? Nothing—except for that tiny little misread of John 10:10. I just assumed that since I was doing my part, God would do his and bless me.

I was going all "Prayer of Jabez" on everybody, but instead of making it about God, I was making it about me. And that's not a good place to be.

Remember earlier how I talked about how bad it is to try to find God in the circumstances? Well, I took it a step further and tried to confirm my faith in the circumstances.

The first major blow came when the band made a lineup change, going from a five-piece to a four-piece band. This was devastating and traumatic on so many levels. The five of us had been a band of brothers for over thirteen years. Early on, someone had prayed over us the verse about David using five smooth stones to slay Goliath, just as there are five members of Third Day.

But then there were four of us.

Surprisingly, though, it worked. After a couple of rough shows, we figured out how to present ourselves as a four-piece band. We had some rocking shows not long after, including an amazing tour with Switchfoot.

Maybe this had nothing to do with my relationship with God, or the band's relationship with God, or any kind of blessing-related stuff. Maybe it was that God was in a relationship with all of us as individuals and not as a band.

Then the Dove Awards rolled around. We were scheduled to play "Revelation," the title track and my favorite song from our new album. Even better, the song had a big old solo at the end. I was so excited for us to show off our new four-piece format in grand fashion.

We did our soundcheck and it sounded huge. This was going to be our moment.

Then our performance slot came around. I nervously checked my gear and it worked like a champ. This was going to be epic!

"Revelation" starts with Mac singing and playing acoustic and Scotty playing on piano. Then the whole band kicks in and we start flat-out bringing it. But when it came time for the band to kick in, I stepped on a couple of my pedals to pull up the sound for that section, then rolled open my volume pedal to unleash the rock.

Nothing.

Not a sound came out of my amp.

Here we were at what was supposed to be the biggest moment of the year, and I was failing epically. All those years of stage fright I had fought so hard to get over came flooding back in waves of anger and shame.

I'm a guitar player. My job is to, well, play the guitar. And when nothing's coming out of my amp, that's a little bit of a problem.

"Help!" I shouted to the side of the stage. My guitar tech came over. He's actually a miracle worker, and was able to repatch some things, and we got a sound to come out of my amp toward the end of the song. The part where I was supposed to play that huge solo. But it sounded small and dinky. It sounded like something was wrong. Because it was.

After the performance we sat silently in the dressing room. Everybody was really supportive and encouraging, but I wasn't buying it. Our manager put it best. He thought I looked like a pitcher who had just gotten shelled in the big game and the other guys were trying to talk me down off the ledge.

Terry, our label president, presenting us with gold plaques for *Christmas Offerings*

Several times that night I prayed a simple and honest prayer: *God, why? If I'm faithful to you, why do you let bad things like this happen?*

My father-in-law has a devotional book written by Zig Ziglar and Ike Reighard. When we're hanging out over there with the family, I will sometimes pick it up and read it. One passage in particular has really helped me in this area of looking for circumstantial rewards for faith.

> Like little children, we may choose to obey God to avoid punishment and experience rewards. While those are certainly strong motivations, God appeals to us to respond in a more mature way, to enjoy a rich relationship instead of just the consequences of punishments and rewards. He reminds us of his role as our Redeemer, who paid a high price to forgive us, and he tells us again about his character as a God of infinite love and blinding holiness. By his actions and by his nature, he has proven that we can trust him.[1]

Yes, God has promised us a lot of amazing things. But for me to expect that if I do *this* then God is going to bless me with *that*, well, that's just me being childish.

Besides, if God promised rewards on earth for being faithful, what about the most faithful of all? Wouldn't they have received all kinds of earthly blessings?

Look at the disciples. They followed Jesus on earth and so were literally the closest to him. After he returned to the Father, the disciples were obedient. They preached the gospel everywhere they went. And they were all, every single one of

1. Zig Ziglar and Dr. Ike Reighard, "Father Knows Best," *The One Year Daily Insights with Zig Ziglar and Dr. Ike Reighard* (Carol Stream, IL: Tyndale House, 2009), February 23.

them, persecuted for it. Beaten. Thrown in jail. And every last one, save for John, was killed for their faith.

And here I was, mad that my guitar didn't work for a TV show. Like that devotional passage said, I was basically acting like a child.

While becoming a dad might have been the moment I grew up emotionally, this was the moment I grew up spiritually.

There's a funny thing about circumstances. They do often work in hindsight. They operate as sort of a confirmation of God working in your life. And, looking back, that divine appointment I had with Steve, and the spiritual awakening that followed, that all really happened. But it took a little trial by fire for me to let go of another of the enemy's little lies and for God to take my faith to another level.

Dan DeHaan hit on a great concept in his second book, *The God You Can Know*. He talks about three kinds of

Third Day Lead Us Back tour, 2016. L–R: David Carr, me, Trevor Morgan, Mac Powell, Scotty Wilbanks, Tim Gibson, and tour pastor Nigel James (Photo credit: Third Day manager Lott Shudde)

Christians: children, adults, and fathers. I had always thought about the "adult" part of it, about being a mature Christian, but I had never thought about this next level of faith. And of course, being a "father" means you have spiritual "offspring" and that there is a spiritual legacy to be had. I want to spend the rest of my life cultivating that legacy.

18

IT MAKES FOR A GREAT STORY

Seek first his kingdom and his righteousness, and all
these things will be given to you as well.

Matthew 6:33

I had the chance to speak to a group of fifth graders recently.
They were about to learn how to figure out their place
in the scheme of things. I told them the story of how I got
hit by the truck, the idea being that a lot of times when we
feel like we're completely off course is actually when God is
putting us in a position where he can work on us. Only later,
after the fact, can we really see what God is doing.

It's as if, as we're living our life and writing our story,
another divine hand is there writing the story with us. That
has definitely been the case for me.

Telling my story again for these kids reminded me of a
lot of things. It reminded me that living life to the fullest as
Jesus talked about is both the easiest and the hardest thing

we can ever do. It is also the most important.

I told them they needed to seek God first. I thought back all those years to the summer after high school, when I committed to God that I was going to seek him first. Looking back over the last couple of decades, I can honestly say

This never gets old—I still feel so humbled and blessed every time I take the stage. (Photo credit: Tracy Kapela)

I've tried. While I haven't always succeeded, that has been the attitude of my heart. And it has made all the difference.

And, of course, I told the kids about finding landmarks in their life. About how if we put our faith in God first then all these other things will flow out of that. People will come into our lives who will help us through. We will see our gifts and talents through the lens of faith and realize the reason God put us exactly right here, right now. These simple

Mac and I bringing the rock to Chattanooga, 2016

things will lift us up during the times we are down and feel we don't deserve to breathe the same air as everyone else. They will keep us humble when we are up and we want to claim credit for ourselves. We realize that it is all God's. Most importantly, whatever happens, we are God's. It is an amazing way to live.

● ● ●

Lately the clock has reappeared for me. When my dad died I thought I would never forget him, and I haven't. *Except.* Except I have now lived longer without him than I did with him. There are so many years in between. So many new memories to keep up with alongside the old.

I have begun to realize that Abbie will only be home with us for a few more years, and when she leaves for college our family will never be the same again. I also know that none of us are getting any younger, that just as my dad had no idea how long he was going to live, none of us do.

I think back to what the doctor told my parents just a few months before Dad died, that nobody knows how long anyone is going to live. At the time I had taken this as good news, but in hindsight I think the doctor was just stating a universal truth. I was sixteen years old when Dad died. It feels like I've blinked and now I'm forty-four. It seems like I'll blink again, and that's kind of it.

Nobody knows how long we have left together. So we've got to make the most of what God has given us for today.

I want my girls to know that they have a dad who loves them no matter what. I make great effort to have fun with them, to make life fun for them, and to capture those little, fleeting moments with the same sense of wonder we'd have capturing lightning bugs in a jar.

I think that's why Jesus told us to seek first the kingdom of God. Because he's given us so much today that it's all we need to focus on. We're so blessed to overflowing that, if we're doing it right, it's all we really can focus on anyway.

● ● ●

Backstage at Red Rocks, 2015

Stephanie and the girls came in the door the other day, and everybody was laughing. They had been out running errands and they drove by that intersection on Hurt Road where my accident happened. Stephanie told the girls all about it, and Kitty seemed to get the biggest kick out of it. When they got home, she had to tell me all about it, as if I had never been there or heard about it.

"Daddy! Mommy said you got hit by a truck, and that you were selling doughnuts, and the guy's name was Mr. Coffee."

"That's right, sweetie."

"And you got hurt and the name of the road was Hurt Road. It sounds like a story."

"You're right. I guess it does."

"Ooh, Daddy! Do you want to catch lightning bugs?"

"Sure," I said.

"Mommy, can you come too?"

"Of course."

We got Ozzy, our dog, and we all went outside. We chased after lightning bugs. We even caught a couple and put them in a jar. For some reason this made Ozzy bark a lot. And the more he barked the more we laughed. It had been a beautiful, sunny day that gives over into one of those perfect summer nights, not unlike my memories of Hollydale all those years ago. It seems like forever ago, on one hand. But on the other hand, it feels like it just happened.

I know we haven't found happily ever after. There are still difficult times ahead. But in learning to trust God in

Capturing moments with my girls: the Lees' Christmas, 2016

the moment, in seeking him first, we've found something better. I hope my girls look back on moments like these like I look back on my early days. I hope they are finding those same landmarks I found so early on from my mom. And from my dad.

Not a day goes by that I don't think about it and wonder. I wonder how things would have been different if my life hadn't taken the strange detour that it did. If high school had been normal. If Dad were still around. But I know that because things happened the way they did, I got to this place right here, and it's a good one.

It will make for a great story one day. But for now, it's just a moment. And that's all it needs to be.

Mark Lee is a founding member and guitarist for the award-winning Christian rock band Third Day, with thirteen albums and total sales approaching eight million. An accomplished songwriter ("Sky Falls Down," "Alien," "Show Me Your Glory," and more), Lee has also written for *CCM Magazine*, *Guideposts for Teens*, and others. While balancing touring with life as a husband and father, he earned his BA in Christian studies from Grand Canyon University. He lives with his family outside Atlanta, Georgia.

THIRDDAY.COM

f /THIRDDAY t /THIRDDAY /THIRDDAY